Soccer
Technique & Tactics

ﾗAT

D0453358

Ｚ

Erich Kollath

SOCCER
TECHNIQUE & TACTICS

Meyer & Meyer Sport

Original title:
Fußball – Technik und Taktik
– Aachen: Meyer und Meyer Verlag, 1998
Translated by Paul D. Chilvers-Grierson

British Library Cataloguing in Publication Data
A catalogue for this book is available from the British Library

Kollath, Erich:
Soccer – Technique & Tactics / Erich Kollath. [Transl.: Paul D. Chilvers-Grierson].
– Oxford : Meyer & Meyer Sport (UK) Ltd., 2000
ISBN 1-84126-016-9

© 2000 by Meyer & Meyer Sport (UK) Ltd.
Oxford, Aachen, Olten (CH), Vienna, Québec,
Lansing/Michigan, Adelaide, Auckland, Johannesburg, Budapest
Member of the World
Sportpublishers' Association

Cover photo: Bongarts Sportfotografie GmbH, Hamburg
Cover design: Walter Neumann, N&N Design-Studio, Aachen
Cover and type exposure: frw, Reiner Wahlen, Aachen
Editorial: Dr. I. Jaeger, Aachen, John Coghlan, Paul Cooper
Printed and bound in Germany
by Druckpunkt Offset GmbH, Bergheim
ISBN 1-84126-016-9
e-mail: verlag@meyer-meyer-sports.com

Contents

Acrobatic shooting technique

Introduction

This book was written for all those interested in soccer generally and who in particular want to learn about the technique and tactics of the game. These people include both those in training and those already active as coaches, instructors and teachers as well as active players.

As the title indicates, the emphasis in this book is on the technique and tactics of soccer. It was further developed from the book "Fußballtechnik in der Praxis" published in 1991 by the same publisher, and was comprehensively revised and extended by a main chapter on tactics.

The two areas technique and tactics can be seen as the "pillars" of any sport. There is always a constant interplay between them. No matter which tactics are applied the appropriate technique is always needed for their execution. Only tactics which take into consideration the technical ability of the players can be of any use to a team. At the same time the tactics must always be adapted to the technical possibilities of the players and not vice versa. Any tactic has to be technically feasible, and must not overtax the technical abilities of the players.

For this reason we will first go into soccer technique in depth. After introductory notes, individual movements without the ball, towards the ball and with the ball will be covered. The details on application in the game, as well as on technique, are followed by a comprehensive presentation of exercise and game forms. After this, soccer tactics are covered. Notes on the tactics of the individual player positions, on group tactics, and the tactics of attacking and defensive play, together with practical examples, sketches and photos contribute to providing a clear presentation of this area. In the appendix, external factors influencing soccer technique, as well as application areas for experimental analyses, are listed to complement these details.

To highlight them better in the text, exercise and game forms are marked with a black dot, general notes with an arrow. To make reading easier, gender-neutral formulation is used.

I wish all readers great enjoyment while reading this book, and success in the game when putting the many practical suggestions into effect.

Erich Kollath

I SOCCER TECHNIQUE

Before individual soccer tactics are dealt with, there are a number of aspects to address which are closely connected with soccer technique. These include remarks on the significance of soccer technique, notes on learning and coaching it, general information on the methodology of technique training, as well as observations on the interplay between technique and the other factors determining play. First, however, we will paraphrase what is meant by the term "technique" in this book: *technique in soccer comprises all movements selected to solve a certain task while observing the rules.*

1 The Significance of Soccer Technique

Soccer is, with certainty, one of the games in which technique can be attributed a dominating role. A major part of the attractiveness of this team sport is due to the "technical players", i.e. players with above average feeling for the ball. If such abilities of individual participants are placed at the service of the whole team, a foundation stone for success is laid.

Owing to the rules system, soccer technique has hardly changed in the last hundred years. Nevertheless, nobody can deny that it is in a constant process of transformation.

A game which is increasingly physical, faster or tactically varied, requires the techniques necessary for this: thus close coverage requires mastery of fair barging and tackling, a faster game tempo calls for quicker execution of all movements and a strong game down the flanks requires mastery of accurate centre crosses.

Greater value must be placed on maintaining techniques already learnt as well as on acquiring new techniques. For this, talent or skill with the ball already present, is certainly an important prerequisite. It must not be overlooked, however, that even the most naturally gifted player needs constant training. Elegant ball control, seemingly effortless dribbling skills, or a hard and well-placed goal strike are not managed by the talented alone, but by the player who also trains diligently.

The Significance of Soccer Technique

Ancient ball game exercise (left)

Soccer player in 1920 (right)

1.1 Learning and Training Soccer Technique

This is a very broad topic and has been the subject of numerous studies, especially from a theoretical point of view. As this book is more practically oriented, details on this will be limited to aspects that seem significant. First of all these include the accepted division into three age-related training levels:

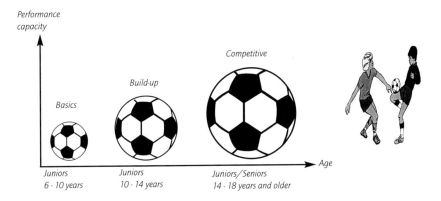

Development of performance capacity

Basic Training

It is accepted as proven that primary school age (6-10 years) offers the best prerequisites for learning sporting techniques. This age-range of juniors should be offered an array of exercise and game forms as diverse as possible in order to improve their feeling for the ball. Much attention should be paid to learning basic techniques such as ball control, dribbling and goal strikes in varied forms.

Action of an eight year-old player

Build-up Training

At this level, which covers a period of about four years, the emphasis is definitely on further developing technique. Whereas the pre-puberty phase (10-12 years) offers the best prerequisites for this, in the first phase of puberty (12-14 years) hampered learning ability must be reckoned with. Generally training of this age-group has more soccer-specific elements. Differing rates of growth and biological immaturity can lead to very different states of development and performance in a team from one year; close observation is required of the coach.

Action of a twelve year-old player

Competitive Training

This last section begins with the second phase of puberty (about 14-17 years for boys, 13 -16 years for girls) and is characterised by almost equally balanced consideration of technique and fitness while at the same time covering tactics. Here technique is once again further developed considerably as a result of increased strength and speed ability. This leads both to economisation as well as stabilisation. Technique becomes more individual and matures to become a personal style. The coach must keep an eye out for movement errors which can „creep in" and are very difficult to correct later. To achieve top performances, the player must be able to apply his techniques variably according to the situation.

Action of a 17 year-old player

1.2 Notes on the Methodology of Technique Training

If certain soccer movement sequences are to be deliberately learnt or improved, then certain conditions must be considered in the course of training: these include among others:

➤ The highest degree of attentiveness and concentration both on the part of the coach and of the players.

➤ The particular exercises must always be carried out in an unfatigued state, i.e. best directly after a general and ball-related warm-up.

➤ The coach should use clear and simple language adapted to his players (children, adolescents or adults).

➤ The practical demonstration of the technique being covered must be done clearly and should at the same time train the participants' ability to observe in a focused manner.

➤ Typical movement errors should also be demonstrated, and in each case the players should give their opinion on correcting the errors.

➤ Means of increasing learning motivation, such as praise and criticism or a call for self-initiative are neglected much too often.

When training technique the selection of particular measures must be strongly oriented to the age-level of the soccer players. Thus in basic training preference should be given to exercise and game forms suitable for children. In the following build-up training the coach usually has to use different measures because of the varying degrees of maturity of the youngsters. If the stability of technique is to be checked, in competitive training this can be done now and again through variation of external conditions: these include, among others, a training:

➤ on unaccustomed ground (artificial grass or cinder instead of grass field),
➤ with poor playing field conditions (unevenness, very hard or soft surface, no pitch markings),
➤ on pitches with unusual dimensions (short, wide or narrow, long playing field),
➤ in unpleasant weather (rain, fog, strong wind, high temperatures) or
➤ at a level of requirements not announced in advance (a longer duration, greater length of exercise, higher intensity) or
➤ with atypical balls (extremely large/small, heavy/light, hard/soft balls – within the region of variation allowed by the rules).

In well-balanced doses such difficulties can only lead to further strengthening of playing skills if technique is already solidly mastered previously.

1.3 Technique and Other Factors Determining the Game

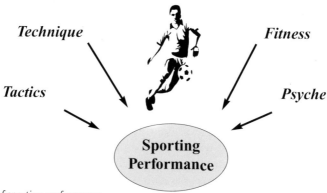

Factors of sporting performance

The emphasis in this book is on soccer technique and tactics. At the same time it is by no means overlooked that in addition to these there are other performance components. We will now briefly address the factors involved and the connections between them.

The Significance of Soccer Technique

Fitness

This means the general physical performance capacity of an athlete. It is closely linked with the biomotor forms of physical demands: strength, speed ability, endurance, co-ordination and flexibility (dexterity). Without a foundation of fitness every technique is imperfect. The difficulty lies in co-ordinating technique and fitness at the various age-levels. It is not possible to give a generally valid recommendation on this, this must be decided by the coach himself – always in relationship to his team. The following can be used as a rough guide: in basic training the above mentioned five forms of physical demands should contribute to a diverse general physical education, and the basic techniques should be learnt. In build-up training perfecting technical skills definitely dominates, additionally conditions are favourable for the improvement of speed ability and endurance. In competitive training finally, technique and fitness can be considered almost equally and further developed with a view to specialisation. Unfortunately all too often strength, speed ability and endurance are coached more than ball skills, which can only lead to decreased performance in the medium and longer term.

Psyche

This last-named but in no way to be underestimated, aspect comprises the mental abilities of a player. A soccer player's ability to increase his technical and also his tactical performance ability is dependent to no small degree on his ability to think. In this respect varying demands are made in the various age categories. In basic training the learning of new movements places demands on the children's concentration, perception and observation abilities. Practically, it must be taken into consideration that one can only expect increased attentiveness amongst young players for a limited time; in between they must be given the opportunity e.g. of free play with the ball. The further development of technique in build-up training can also be put down to the ability to precisely and mentally process movements that have been explained and demonstrated. An emphasis in competitive training is placed on encouraging technically mature players to practise concentratedly, not by always placing the same demands on them, but by challenging them in constantly changing ways. Players should carry out training "consciously", which also involves occasional explanatory comments and theoretical observations by the coach. Taking the psychological factors mentioned into consideration also contributes to promoting frequently lacking virtues such as "playing intelligence".

2 Movements without the Ball

Although every soccer player tries to get possession of the ball as often as possible, for much of the game he moves without the ball. This occurs in various forms of movement, depending on the situation. As a rule these are differentiated by whether the player moves at a high or low tempo. The following illustration shows a rough division.

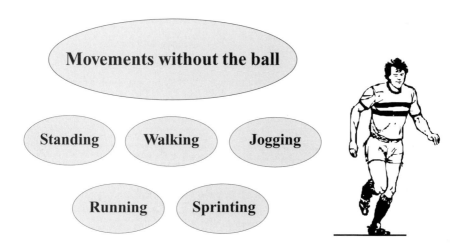

Division of movements without the ball

2.1 Running

2.1.1 Application and Technique

As soccer is indisputably a "running game", for some time now analyses of running distances have been made. These kind of values characterise the requirement profile and are also helpful for fitness training. They are very much dependent, however, on the chosen playing system, tactics, and not least on the position of the particular player. In the literature data about running distances during the last thirty years is known. Average values of defence, midfield and attack players can be found in the following illustration.

Soccer Technique

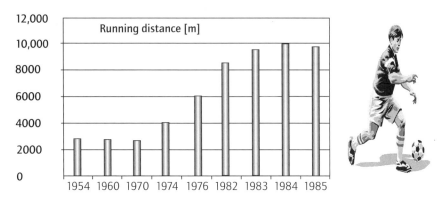

Running distances of soccer players over a period from 1954 to 1985 (average values)

As can be seen from this illustration, the distances run by soccer players have almost tripled from the mid-Fifties (3.5 km) to the mid-Eighties (10 km). From this can be seen how changed playing systems in combination with intensive training have led to increased running requirements of players. As already mentioned, the values in each case vary considerably from player to player. Here are some examples: in the early Sixties the star forwards of the time, Garrincha and di Stefano, covered 2.8 km and 4.4 km respectively per game. In a UEFA Cup game in 1984 a distance of around 8.1 km was determined for K. H. Rummenigge (Inter Milano), while midfield player T. von Heesen (Hamburger SV) even ran 14.2 km. The fact that in today's high tempo soccer the referee is also faced with high running demands should not go unmentioned: depending on the course of the game he has to cover 8-11 km per match.

In order to better evaluate the most certainly informative data on distances run for practical fitness and technique training, additional details on the duration of the individual types of running are necessary. Here too data is available, which comes from top European teams in the mid-Eighties. It can be seen in the next illustration.

These average figures show a picture that will certainly surprise many readers: for more than half of the playing time an outfield player is walking; almost 80 minutes are spent walking and jogging! If you add up the times for running and sprinting, this totals only about seven minutes! As was to be expected, there were differences between the various playing positions: in comparison to the defending and attacking players, the midfield

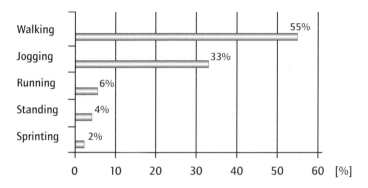

Percentage duration of various types of movement in the course of a soccer match (average values)

players spend more time jogging and less time standing or walking when they could recover. Thus the rapid types of movement felt to be strenuous only makeup a small part of total playing time between them.

The simultaneous observation of distances covered in the relevant velocity areas provides an interesting combination. The following division applies to an average running distance of 10.4 km in a match:

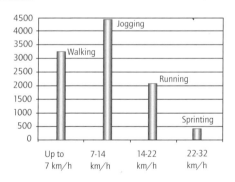

Distances covered with corresponding running velocities (average values)

The highest of the four columns applies to the velocity area between 7 and 14 km/h; at jogging tempo the player covers a distance of 4.5 km altogether. Faster running at between 14 and 22 km/h still adds up to about 2 km, and the sum of all sprints with speeds between 22 and 32 km/h is a distance of 450 m.

For effective execution of running movement the following general comments apply:

- The soccer player must adapt his running technique to the changing game situation and always be ready to change speed and direction.
- For this the player's body should be bent slightly lower than e.g. during the more upright running of a track and field athlete.
- A lower body posture can be achieved by slightly bending the ankles, knees and hips.
- The upwards and downwards movements of the body when running must be minimal.
- The push-off from the ground must be more forwards and sideways than upwards.
- The arm movements serve to increase running speed, to stabilise balance and to prepare for body contact with the opponent.

For the improvement of sprinting ability in particular the following should be noted:

- Acceleration from a slower running movement has advantages over a sprint from a standing position.
- In the starting position the feet should not be parallel but rather in an open stride position.
- The player's weight should be moved forward by slightly bending the upper body in order to be able to push off from the balls of the feet more forcefully.
- A lowering of the body by bending slightly increases the accelerating distance before the push-off.
- With a longer acceleration distance more muscle strength, and thus also higher velocity, can be developed.
- Slippery ground makes it necessary to adjust running technique, whereby wearing longer studs reduces the danger of slipping.

Training general endurance through slow to medium-fast runs is a necessary basis for running training. In addition short, fast accelerations over about 5-30 m in competition-like form must be given consideration. Training speed ability is equally important for all parts of the team, i.e. both for the attack and the defence. It must be an objective of running training to achieve fast recovery after highly intensive sprints. When training speed endurance, the ratio of load to recovery time must always be carefully adjusted to the performance state of the players. Loads that are too high in short intervals restrict technique, reduce the ability to concentrate, promote faulty performance and also lengthen recovery time.

2.1.2 Exercise and Game Forms

- At first intensive warming-up with runs of lower and medium intensity.
- Then diverse gymnastics, especially loosening and stretching of the leg and torso muscles as well as a targeted stretching.
- Runs with quick raising of the knees and pushing off from the heels.
- From jogging speed, fast accelerations over 5-30 m straight ahead, forwards to the right and left.
- Sudden acceleration from various positions such as crouching, kneeling, sitting, lying on the stomach or back.
- Fast change from forwards to backwards running.
- From jogging speed, take off to the side or the rear.

(see photo series on page 22)

- Accelerating and speed runs.
- Downhill and uphill runs.
- Shadow running.
- Getting away from fellow players.
- Zigzag running around poles.
- Running with knees raised over poles.
- Pursuit running around poles.

(see photo series on page 23)

- **Tag Game**
  The player tries to tag one of the other players. Determine the area to hit, e.g. only back or arm (leg) on the right or the left side of the body.

- **Throw-off Game**
  Like the previous game form, the throwing to a certain part of the body is now done with a (soft) ball.

- **Catching Game**
  At a signal all players try to reach the opposite side of the playing field. The catcher may only run backwards, the others only forwards; include body feints and fast changes of running direction.

It is very important to ensure breaks between the individual speed exercises. Walking or slow jogging, relaxing gymnastics or light activity with the ball can be recommended as a bridge between exercises.

Jogging straight ahead

Taking-off to the side

Taking-off to the rear

Shadow running

Getting away from a fellow player

Zigzag running around poles

Running with knees raised over poles

Pursuit running around poles

Movements towards the ball

3 Movements towards the Ball

In the case of movements towards the ball, players try to tackle the opponent and get possession of the ball themselves. The techniques here are mainly those of the one-on-one. Unfortunately this area is neglected much too often in training. Thus one finds in all performance classes many players who show unmistakable weaknesses in this respect. Unskilled moving towards the ball is either without success, leads to a foul or even involves the risk of injuries. It therefore makes sense to go into the technique of moving towards the ball in more depth. In such actions, two conditions must be fulfilled: on the one hand the opponent is to be successfully tackled, i.e. separated from the ball, and on the other hand the rules must be kept to. The techniques which are attributed to this area can be seen in the following illustration.

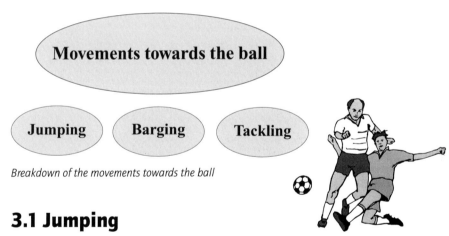

Breakdown of the movements towards the ball

3.1 Jumping

3.1.1 Application and Technique

In many situations a soccer player is forced to execute typical movements in combination with a jump. This applies to a large degree to the goalkeeper. Outfield players in all positions, however, must also jump in many actions, such as e.g.
➤ when attempting to win the ball in the air,
➤ when receiving high balls,
➤ when passing on balls passed high, or
➤ with many headers.

In combination with the execution of such movements the following demands are placed on the player:

➤ Estimation of the trajectory of the ball and/or the movements of the opponent.
➤ Timing of one's own movements to coincide with those of the opposing player and/or the ball.
➤ Successful execution of the actual movement taking into consideration the game situation and the rules of the one-on-one.

In order to get the advantage in a one-on-one, in most cases it is necessary to reach the greatest possible height when jumping. In soccer jumps are executed from two different starting movements:

➤ from a standing position, almost exclusively with a two-legged take-off and
➤ with a run up, both with a one-legged and a two-legged take-off.

Usually the player cannot freely decide which form he will use. That inevitably results from the game situation of the moment. Frequently too there is not much time to prepare the jump. With this in mind the following general advice on jumping technique can be given:

➤ If possible the take-off should be executed using both legs. This leads to a distribution of power between both legs which is both more economical and usually leads to a greater jumping height.
➤ Before the take-off itself there should be a preparatory downward movement of the body. This pre-tenses the leg muscles which can then develop greater power. In combination with a longer acceleration distance this also helps to reach a greater jumping height.
➤ Further support is given to the jump by swinging the arms (and the swinging leg in the case of a one-legged take-off). In addition the arms stabilise the body in the air in relationship to the opponent also jumping, whereby, however, it must be ensured that the rules are kept to.
➤ Jumping with a run-up has advantages over jumping from a standing position. The energy of the running movement can be used for the take-off and in striving for a greater jumping height. Forward velocity, however, must be sufficiently braked to avoid jumping on or knocking over the opponent.

We point out again that not all comments on aiding jumping technique can be realised in every game situation. Nevertheless they should receive appropriate attention.

As the previous remarks have already made clear, in addition to technique, the success of a jumping movement also depends to a great extent on the biomotor factor "strength". In accordance with the subject of this book, however, we will not go into special strength training for soccer players with the aid of weights, or strength machines. The following practical examples can be carried out in training sessions without costly aids. When carrying them out it is important to pay close attention to the execution of the movements previously mentioned.

3.1.2 Exercise Forms

- Initial specific warming-up, in particular loosening and stretching of the leg and torso muscles as well as a running warm-up at a slow jog.
- Leaping run, with emphasised push-off upwards with support from the arms and the swinging leg.
- Jumping run, straight ahead and to the side.
- Imitation of a jumping header, with one- and two-legged take-off.
- Squat and straddle vaults, also with one- and two-legged take-off.
- One-legged jumps, after 3-4 jumps change the jumping leg.
- Two-legged and one-legged jumps over hurdles.
- Jump for header.

(see picture series on page 28)

Above:
Two-legged hurdle jumps

Middle:
One-legged hurdle jumps

Below:
Jump for header

The volume and intensity of such exercises is very much dependent on the age and training state of the players. In between there should be breaks for recovery and for relaxing gymnastics. Vertical jumps from various starting positions, and low jumps from a box, followed by stretch jumps, are suitable for testing jumping height. Objective analyses to determine exactly excessive raising of the body's centre of gravity are possible using contact mats, or strength measuring platforms; see Appendix (pages 141ff.).

3.2 Shoulder Charging

3.2.1 Application and Technique

Because soccer is a physical game almost every one-on-one involves physical contact with the opponent. Both the attacker and the player in possession of the ball employ a measure of shoulder charging. In order to carry out this action according to the rules the following should be noted:

➤ The arms must touch the upper body.
➤ The shoulder comes in contact with the opponent.
➤ It is forbidden to purposely knock over the opponent or push him away with one's hands.
➤ Shoulder charging is only allowed when struggling for the ball.

If the player in ball possession sees that it is intended to get the ball off him by shoulder charging, he should react as follows:

➤ Shield the ball from the opponent if possible, i.e. place the own body between the ball and the opponent.
➤ Move the shoulder on the side away from the ball towards the opponent.
➤ Consciously tense arm and torso muscles shortly before and during body contact.
➤ Bend at the knees slightly, as slightly lowering the body makes it easier to keep one's balance.
➤ At the moment of being shoulder charged, move your weight to the leg nearest the opponent.

The last point in particular is very important from a movement technique point of view: if you are briefly forced outwards by a shoulder contact with the opponent, you can quickly compensate this again with a push-off from the outer leg. If, however, your body weight is already on the outer leg when you are pushed, you cannot catch yourself quickly when the opponent uses his body forcefully. As a result you lose your balance, are diverted from your intended course and usually lose the ball.

Experienced players occasionally manage to get out of the way of the opponents' body by means of a sudden change of running speed, direction or a clever feint, letting him run on into empty space. Nevertheless, shoulder charging is often unavoidable and for the following reasons should therefore be given due consideration in training:

➤ There is necessarily a strengthening in particular of the arm and torso muscles, which are much too frequently underdeveloped in soccer players in comparison to their strong leg muscles.

➤ Players lose their hesitation about the one-on-one and learn to make use of their body more consciously.

➤ Appropriate exercises, also in a playful form, are enjoyable for the players and contribute to variety in training.

3.2.2 Exercise Forms

Initial specific warming-up, especially of the torso and leg muscles.

- **Shoulder Charging while Running**
  Two players run parallel to each other and through fair shoulder charging try to get each other away from their straight running direction.

- **Shoulder Charging while Jumping**
  Two players simultaneously carry out a stretching jump and try to put their partner off balance while in the air with fair shoulder charging.

- **Shoulder Charging during One-on-one**
  a) The attacker harries the player in ball possession with fair shoulder charging, without getting the ball, however.
  b) In combination with fair shoulder charging the attacker tries to get possession of the ball.
  c) The player in ball possession tries to avoid the one-on-one of the shoulder charging opponent with clever feints and evasive action.

- **Pushing Competition**
  Two players stand shoulder-to-shoulder at the level of the 16 m line and try to push each other about 2 m away from the line with fair shoulder charging.

(see picture series on page 31)

Movements towards the Ball

Above:
Shoulder charging during one-on-one

Below:
Pushing competition

- **Shoulder Charging when Centring**
  The player with the ball dribbles from a wing position from the centre line towards the opponents' goal and tries, despite hindrance (partly active/active) by a shoulder charging opponent, to centre the ball in front of the goal.

- **Shoulder Charging during 1 plus three-on-three**
  In free play in a marked-off area with a neutral passer, the player with the ball may only kick-off after he has won a one-on-one against a shoulder charging defender.

Such exercises are justified both in junior and in senior training. With their diversity they contribute to improving one-on-one behaviour in competitive games. They can be placed either at the end of warming-up or at the beginning of the main part, as a priority in combination with the training feature "defence activity".

3.3 Tackling

3.3.1 Application and Technique

"Tackling" is a collective term for various movements aimed at separating the opponent from the ball. The correct execution of tackling places high demands on a player. You have to develop a feeling for the best moment to use this technique and above all you must observe the rules of fairness. Much too frequently bad tackling leads to a foul because the player either goes to the ball too late, or through an uncoordinated movement hits the opponent and causes him to fall. In order to avoid disadvantages resulting from this, improvement of tackling must be a component of technique training for soccer players.

Because the individual forms of tackling are very diverse, it is difficult to provide a comprehensive breakdown. It does, however, seem useful to differentiate roughly between two types: the *block tackle* and the *sliding tackle*.

Block Tackle
Here the defending player moves towards the ball without his body going to the ground.
Objective: To hinder the opponent from carrying out a dribble, a pass, a cross or a shot at goal.

Tackling in a game

Position: The defending player stands in front of or sideways from the person with the ball.

Technique: The defender prevents a pass by blocking the ball with his foot.

The block tackle can be characterised as a typical and certainly the most frequently used defence technique. In the constantly changing game situations the defender must adapt to the opponent and the ball again and again.

Sliding Tackle

With this form of tackling the defending player slides towards the ball and his body touches the ground. It is always used when the opponent has the ball so far from the defender that the latter can no longer reach it with a block tackle. Depending on the position in relationship to the opponent, one must differentiate between a number of variants:

a) Sliding Tackle with the Sole of the Foot

Objective: To separate the opponent from the ball.

Position: The defending player stands in front of or sideways from the person with the ball.

Technique: With a classical "straddle" the ball is played away to the side with the sole of the foot. The body posture is similar to a hurdling crouch.

b) Sliding Tackle with the Inner or Whole Instep

Objective: To separate the opponent from the ball.

Position: The defending player is at the same level, or usually slightly behind the person with the ball.

Technique: The ball is played away to the side with the inner or whole instep of the leg away from or the leg close to the opponent. The sliding phase on the ground is longer than the form just described, whereby the outside of the lower leg is in contact with the ground.

c) Sliding Tackle with the Inside of the Foot

Objective: To gain possession of the ball oneself through tackling.

Position: The defending player runs next to or usually slightly behind the person with the ball.

Technique: The defender slides towards the ball as in the form just described, but this time he presses it to the ground with the inside of his foot. Thus the running attacking player can no longer drive the briefly blocked ball onwards. The defender gets up quickly and secures the ball just won.

(see picture series on the next page)

The sliding tackle should only be used when there are no other defensive options available. From a tactical point of view it is advantageous to force the attacker beforehand into an unfavourable position with regard to the goal. In this way it is possible for another defence player to move in if the tackle is unsuccessful. For the referee it is often extremely difficult to clearly differentiate between a legal and an unfair tackle as often in such situations both players end up on the ground. Mastering faultless technique makes it easier for the neutral person to decide whether the attacker was separated from the ball by fair use of the body or by an illegal action.

Successful execution of a sliding tackle is very much dependent on the ground conditions. A damp grass field is most suitable. Because of the danger of light injuries such as grazes it is not advisable to use the sliding tackle on hard pitches.

Block tackle

Sliding tackle on a player dribbling

Blocking the ball in a sliding tackle

3.3.2 Exercise Forms

- Initial specific warming-up with gymnastic exercises to loosen and stretch the hip muscles such as e.g.
  - Swinging the leg backwards and forwards (normally and figures of eight); swinging sideways and imitation of a shot at hip level.
  - Straddle angle stand; shift the hips horizontally to the right and left; open your leg out to the side in a crouch; sit cross-legged; hurdle crouch, bending the torso forwards, backwards and sideways.
  - Take up the sliding tackle position from a standing situation, after a few start-up steps and from jogging tempo.

- **Sliding Tackle on a Stationary Ball**
  From a slow running up movement shoot away to the side several stationary balls in a row using sliding tackles. In doing so alternately use the right and left leg and hit the ball with the sole of the foot, the inside or the whole instep.

  (see picture series on the opposite page)

- **Sliding Tackle on a Player Dribbling**
  Separate the slowly dribbling player from the ball using sliding tackles from the right and left sides. The defender only acts when the ball is briefly "exposed" and is not protected by the leg close to the opponent.

- **Blocking the Ball**
  First block stationary then dribbled balls with your foot or lower leg in such a way that after the action you are in possession of the ball.

- **Sliding Tackles with a Time Limit**
  In as fast a sequence as possible, use sliding tackles to get several balls placed next to cones into a marked zone.

- **Sliding Tackles in Games One-on-one**
  The defender tries to separate the attacker dribbling towards the goal from the ball by means of a sliding tackle.

- **Sliding Tackle with Targeted Pass**
  Two players stand opposite each other in two goals marked by cones. The ball passed diagonally from the partner is diverted towards the opposing goal with a sliding tackle.

Stretching exercises for sliding tackles

Sliding tackle with a stationary ball

- **Dribbling against Sliding Tackles**
  Attacker and defender take off after a through pass. In doing so the forward should move the ball across a target line in a controlled dribble, and the defending player tries to disrupt him with a sliding tackle.

- **Block and Sliding Tackles in Games Four-on-Four towards a Goal**
  Two defenders disrupt four attackers outside the penalty area with block tackling only, the other two within the penalty area with sliding tackles only. Shots at goal are only allowed after a successful one-on-one.

Before the various forms of tackling are used in game forms, solid mastery of technique in preparatory exercise forms is necessary. In the course of this there should be a progression from initially slowly executed movements without an opponent to applications in competition-like situations. The objective always remains to separate the opponent from the ball with a fair action.

Action towards the ball

4 Movements with the Ball

After movement without the ball – running – and movements towards the ball – jumping, shoulder charging and tackling – we now turn to what is certainly the most important part of soccer technique: movements with the ball. Mastering the ball in the various game situations is a central topic in the technique training of every soccer player. Not only the junior just getting started is concerned with this. Top league players also devote part of their training time to constant improvement and consolidation of their technique. The following overview shows which techniques or technical-tactical actions are included amongst movements with the ball.

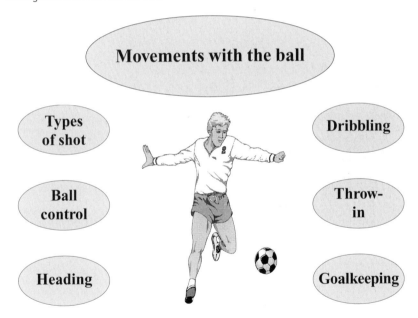

Breakdown of movements with the ball

Shooting can be seen as an elementary soccer movement. The various types of shot are covered individually below. First, however, we will look at the motion sequence of general shots which will provide a number of helpful tips for practical situations.

Goal kick

Movements with the Ball

4.1 Basic Information on the Goal Shooting Movement

Shooting is a procedure which takes place more and more automatically with increasing game experience. With diverse and intensive training the strength of shots and their accuracy can be greatly improved. This objective is pursued e.g. by all top league players, although with obviously varying success. Although they train with about the same frequency, there are only a few real "specialists" among them who can shoot particularly hard and accurately. Why is that? The players themselves cannot explain this conclusively. Nor can the most experienced coach, observing very closely, determine what makes up a hard shot taking place in fractions of a second. Here the findings of sports science can be of help. Whether or not a player is able to achieve above average shooting strength depends on two factors: muscular conditions and shooting technique.

Shooting movement

Muscular conditions

Shooting technique

– upper body
– standing leg
– shooting leg
– ball contact

Factors influencing the shooting movement

There is an interaction between the muscular conditions of a player and his shooting technique. The externally invisible shooting technique is in turn dependent to a large degree on the movement of the upper body, the standing and shooting legs and on ball contact.

Muscular Conditions

A high degree of strength in the muscles involved in the shooting movement is always an essential prerequisite. From an individually varying point onwards, however, an improvement

41

of shot hardness can no longer be achieved even with the most intensive strength training. This is because of the particular compilation of the muscles which consist of "fast" and "slow" twitch fibres and a "mixed type". For those in the field it is useful to know that on the whole this muscle fibre ratio, which varies from player to player, is predetermined by nature. It is possible, however, to cause a thickening of the "fast" fibres and a transformation of part of the "mixed type" into "fast" fibres with special training. If at the same time the working together of the individual muscle bundles is improved, shooting strength can be increased further still. It will, however, hardly be possible to turn a player with an excess of "slow" fibres into a specialist for powerful goal shots.

Shooting Technique

Upper Body

Because the upper body makes up about half of a player's total body mass, the movement of this body segment is very significant for shooting technique. In many soccer training books the correct execution of a hard and well-placed shot is linked with a slight bending forward of the upper body. On the basis of many of my own analyses of the movement of adolescent and adult soccer players, this rule cannot be generally supported. It turned out that e.g. hard shots were also carried out with the upper body leaning slightly backwards, which did not necessarily lead to uncontrolled shots above the goal. If the player is able to stabilise his upper body in a moderately backward-leaning position and to hit the ball in the middle, this can in no way be called faulty. This applies both to youth and to top league players. Among juniors (12-14) in particular it was found that a slight leaning back of the upper body aided a steeper take-off of the ball. At this age-level in particular it is very difficult for the goalkeeper to control high flying balls because of the unfavourable relationship of body size to goal size. Therefore a leaning back of the upper body when shooting the ball should in no way be always considered faulty.

Standing Leg

In a similar way to the torso the standing leg contributes to stabilising the body when shooting. The foot should be placed near the ball and the toe should point in the direction the player is aiming at. In particular in the case of a shot after fast dribbling, the motion of the standing leg contributes to a high degree to achieving a hard shot. Linked with the placing of the standing leg to prepare a shot is a stemming effect which favours fast swinging forward of the kicking leg. This move requires good timing, however, and above all powerful leg extensor muscles. Excessive bending at the knee of the standing leg is unfavourable and often occurs among muscularly poorly developed adolescent players.

Movements with the Ball

Shooting Leg

The velocities of the thigh, lower leg and foot of the kicking leg must be synchronised with each other with regard to their movement sequences. With a shot at over 100 km/h the swing to the ball only lasts about six hundredths of a second, the contact time of foot and ball is less than one hundredth of a second. Here the human eye is not able to register details. High frequency films have shown that the segments of the kicking leg influence each other mutually. At first it is important to quickly brake the thigh in preparation for the shot. The better a player manages this, the less power he needs for the following acceleration of the lower leg and foot. Thus for a hard shot you not only need strongly accelerating but also "braking" muscles. To prevent possible injuries the front extensor and rear flexor muscles of the thigh for example should be at almost equal strength ratio to each other. The following illustration shows how quickly the kicking leg moves in a hard shot by national German player Lothar Matthaeus.

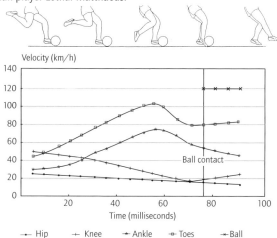

Velocity sequence of hip, knee, ankle and toes during a shot by Lothar Matthaeus (118 km/h)

As you can see, the velocities of the hip and knee constantly decrease from the beginning of the section shown until ball contact. This means that at the beginning of the swinging forward of the kicking leg the thigh is already braked and moves forward more slowly than the lower leg. The ankle and toes on the other hand reach increasingly greater velocities. About one hundredth of a second before hitting the ball the foot reaches its highest velocity, which then decreases rapidly. This can be put down to the use of the knee flexor muscles which are active simultaneously with the knee extensors. In addition the calf muscles are tensed which results in extension of the foot. Because of this brief activity of the thigh, lower leg and foot muscles, the shooting leg already slows down shortly before ball contact. At first sight this may seem unfavourable, but when seen more closely it has one major advantage. For through the simultaneous tensing of the extensor and flexor muscles there is a fixation of the joint. This in turn creates favourable prerequisites for a high level of impulse transmission of the whole body movement to the ball. In order to shoot with above average force it is thus necessary to have fine co-ordination of submovements down to milliseconds.

Ball Contact

Another major prerequisite for achieving as strong a shot as possible is the type of ball contact. This often only lasts less then a hundredth of a second and is also not perceptible to the human eye in detail. Any experienced player, however, can tell by feeling whether or not he has hit the ball properly. It is only possible to make visible how the foot moves during a correct or an incorrect kicking of the ball by using technical measuring devices. An example can be seen in the following illustration.

These photos are high-frequency films with 500 pictures per second. On the photo at the left you can see that the pro hits the ball with his instep according to the book. The amateur on the other hand touches the ball more with the front of the foot which results in conspicuous overstretching. This effect is increased even more through wearing running shoes with very flexible soles. Evaluation of the attempt shown on the right showed that a slow movement of the kicking leg, too great a distance between the standing leg and the ball and an unfavourable contact phase led to a take-off velocity of the previously stationary ball of only 95 km/h. This example illustrates that faulty technique can not

Foot positions during two shooting attempts; left: by German national player Lothar Matthaeus, right: amateur W. P.

only restrict sporting performance. There is also a risk of injury because the foot is extremely overstretched if the ball is hit incorrectly. In accordance with anatomical facts the stronger mid-foot bones of the instep are better suited to transmit great energy to the ball without risk than the weaker toe bones at the front of the foot.

The evaluation of a number of attempts led to the following results of note for practical situations: the greater the foot velocity was before ball contact, the higher the ball velocity was. A short contact time of foot and ball at the point of contact was also typical for hard shot attempts. If the ball was hit more in the area of the front of the foot, this led to lower ball velocities.

The movement of the kicking leg should also be executed in such a way that the foot is moving as fast as possible when it hits the ball. Also, keeping the entire foot stiff during ball contact should be considered equally as important as the often emphasised fixation of the upper ankle joint.

The recommendations here are concentrated on the movement of the kicking leg and were initially considered only with regard to reaching as high a ball velocity as possible. In many game situations the hardness of a shot is also extremely important, such as e.g. a goal kick, a clearing shot from defence or a shot at goal from a great distance. In addition to this, in every case a shot must have a minimum degree of accuracy in order to reach the target. As experience shows, mastery of a really hard and at the same time accurate shot is ideal. In many situations, however, accuracy is at least as important as hardness of the shot. This also applies to shots at goal. It is not always the spectacular shot from a distance that leads to success, many goals are scored from a closer distance with less hard but well-placed shots. This must be taken into account in connection with the following suggestions which apply to youth players especially, but also to amateur seniors.

The following general comments apply to the training of the shooting movement:
- Observe the general indications for executing a shot which are well-known and have just been mentioned briefly.
- Do not try immediately to reach as great a ball velocity as possible.
- Initially, with slow movement of the kicking leg, concentrate on hitting the ball correctly.
- Consciously observe yourself whether you hit the ball properly with the particular part of your foot.
- Ask fellow players to closely observe slowly executed shots and if necessary give advice on corrections.
- With constant correct striking of the ball gradually the velocity of the shooting movement should be increased.

4.2 Typical Errors and Corrections

The Player "Falls Backwards"

An exaggerated backwards position of the upper body when shooting can often be put down to underdeveloped torso muscles. Stomach and gluteal muscles that are too weak, as well as strong hip flexor muscles, favour the development of a hollow back which can often be seen as the cause of problems and injuries in this area. The following exercises are recommended to compensate for this:

- Strengthening of the stomach muscles; e.g. lying on one's back with legs bent up, slightly raise the head and upper body from the ground.
- Strengthening of the gluteal muscles; e.g. bench position, stretch alternating legs out backwards and keep them parallel to the ground.
- Stretching of the hip flexor muscles; e.g. kneeling on one leg with the other leg forward for support, pull up and hold the back leg firmly.
- Stretching of the back extensor muscles; e.g. sitting with stretched out legs grasp your ankles with your hands, or squatting, put your arms around your shins and roll over backwards.

(see photos on page 47)

The Standing Leg Is Bent too much

Such "buckling" also usually results from muscular weaknesses. When shooting while in motion the standing leg has to absorb great external forces as a result of stopping abruptly. In so doing the extensor muscles of the leg are forced to function eccentrically (giving way) to a greater degree. Deficits in this respect can be rectified with the following exercises among others:

- Eccentric strengthening of the lower leg muscles; e.g. through one- or two-legged hopping on the spot with pronounced bending and stretching of the upper ankle joint, or skipping.
- Eccentric strengthening of the thigh muscles; e.g. through low jumps from a low height (20-40 cm) followed by stretched high jumps or squat jumps over small boxes.

Often too much bending of the standing leg occurs in combination with a fall to the ground. In this case the torso and gluteal muscles must also be strengthened.

The Back-swing Movement of the Kicking Leg Is Insufficient

If a hard shot is to be executed, the kicking leg must be swung right back in preparation. This increases the acceleration distance of the foot and pre-tenses the muscle. For this to be

Stretching and strengthening exercises

possible the player must possess a high degree of nimbleness of the joints and elasticity. The following exercises serve to ensure this:

- Put your hand on your team-mates' shoulders and stand next to each other, swinging your leg forwards and backwards, sideways or in figures of eight.
- Swing your leg a long way backwards and forwards, bending the upper body forwards during the forward swing and backwards during the backward swing.
- In the bench position raise your lower leg to the rear, clasp your ankle and pull it up towards your back.
- Place the instep of your bent leg on your kneeling partner's shoulder, pushing your hips forwards and keeping your shoulders back.

Especially when training juniors, often the participants do not see the necessity for such gymnastic exercises. Here it is up to the coach to convince the players in an understandable way of the importance of well-developed body muscles. Loosening, stretching and strengthening exercises must be organised with variety and should be a component of every training session. In this respect the coach must teach his players self-responsibility. They should be put in a position to warm up on their own accord at the beginning of the training or before a game.

(see following photo)

Young players warming up on their own.

In particular it must be considered that strong back and stomach muscles ensure the necessary stability for the shooting movement. Well-developed torso muscles maintain the natural form of the spine and also increase strength in one-on-ones. In order to make sure no imbalance occurs, the muscles at the front and back of the body should be approximately balanced. If, for example, the thigh extensors develop more strength than the thigh flexors, in the long-term the greater load will lead to one-sided use of the knee joint with foreseeable damage from wear. When selecting exercises it must be ensured that muscles already shortened are not additionally strengthened. Rather they must be stretched while the opposite, overstretched muscles need to be strengthened.

5 Types of Goal Shot

Shooting at goal

The breakdown of the various types of shot is based on which part of the foot has contact with the ball. Depending on the game situation and tactical considerations, you use the inside, the inner, outer or whole instep of the foot; only in special cases is the ball played with the sole, the toes or the heel. The following illustration shows the most common shooting techniques.

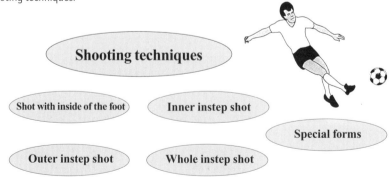

Shooting techniques

Shot with inside of the foot

Inner instep shot

Special forms

Outer instep shot

Whole instep shot

Breakdown of the most important shooting techniques

Types of Goal Shot

The various types of shot make it possible to give the ball the desired direction and velocity: low, medium-high or high, over a short, medium or long distance, kicked hard or "soft" and straight ahead or with spin (side).

5.1 Shot with the Inside of the Foot

5.1.1 Application and Technique

Shot with inside of the foot

The shot with the inside of the foot is a technique used often during the game. It is used for passes over short distances which are meant to be not so much hard as accurate. On uneven and bumpy soccer pitches the inside shot is also frequently used because it provides a high degree of passing certainty and accuracy. The advantage of high precision, however, is matched by a number of disadvantages: on the one hand there are limits to shot hardness, and on the other hand the intended direction of the shot can be recognised early; turning the kicking leg sideways contributes to a disruption of the natural running rhythm and attentive opponents often recognise it as it begins.

The ball is kicked with the inside of the foot which is a large area between the heel bone, inside ankle and big toe joint. The standing leg is set down next to the ball with the long axis pointing in the direction of the shot. The joints of the standing leg are slightly bent in the course of the kicking movement. The upper body remains vertical or leans slightly forwards. Turning the kicking foot outwards is characteristic of the preparatory swing movement. It allows the ball to be hit with the foot turned sideways, the tip of which is slightly raised. If the ball is to be played low and without spin, it must be hit in the centre. Tensing the front and rear lower leg muscles ensures fixation of the upper ankle on ball contact. After the ball has been hit, the movement of the kicking leg no longer influences its trajectory. Nevertheless if possible there should be a follow-through swing of the kicking leg and no abrupt stopping.

Picture series of the shot with the inside of the foot

5.1.2 Exercise and Game Forms

- **Shot with the Inside of the Foot in Teamwork**
  Two partners running slowly pass each other the ball with two contacts or directly. In so doing, the distance between the players is constantly varied between 2 m and 15 m.

- **Concertina**
  Two partners stand opposite each other at a distance of about 15 m and pass each other the ball as directly as possible while moving forward. When the distance is down to only about 2 m, the ball is passed while running backwards.

- **Fan Formation Passing**
  One partner passes the ball from a standing position as directly as possible to a fellow player about 5 m away. He receives the pass alternately half right and half left and returns the ball while running with the right or left inside of the foot.

- **Alternating Cross and Through Pass**
  While running forward two partners alternately pass each other the ball with cross and through passes. After a through pass there is a race to the ball.

- **Passing and Taking-off in a Circle**
  About eight players form a circle and pass each other the ball as directly as possible. After every pass they follow the ball and take up the partner's place.
  Variation: Simultaneous playing with two balls.

- **Passing around Obstacles**
  Obstacles are made with cones, benches, medicine balls or corner flags and freely distributed. Pairs of players pass each other the ball avoiding the obstacles.

- **Field Change**
  4-6 players pass the ball to one another on a field of about 10 x 15 m. After the pass there is a change with a brief acceleration to an adjacent playing field of the same size.

- **Game Three-on-one (Four-on-two) in a Restricted Area**
  On a field of about 10 x 10 m the ball is passed one or two touch in groups of three (four) in the face of disruption by a (two) defender(s). If a pass is unsuccessful, the player swaps with the defence player.

- **Game Four-on-four with two Small Goals**
  On a field of about 30 m x 40 m there is free play using two approx. 3 m wide small goals without goalkeepers. Both in passing and shooting the ball may only be played as a low pass with the inside of the foot.

5.2 Inner Instep Shot

5.2.1 Application and Technique

Whereas the shot with the inside of the foot is mainly used for short passes, the inner instep shot is used for passes over greater distances. Crosses from the wing, diagonal passes and also corners are mainly executed with this technique. It is, however, also frequently used for shooting both from free play and free kicks. This technique also offers the possibility of playing the ball with spin in a way which no other technique does. Use is made of this in free kicks etc., when the ball is to be played around defenders into the goal. With the inner instep shot the player does not move in a straight line, but rather at

Inner instep shot

an angle to the ball. The upper body leans slightly away from the kicking leg. The standing leg is placed next to the ball, the toes point in the direction of the shot. In the course of the swing-back movement there is a bending of the knee and a turning outwards of the hip of the kicking leg. This results in a long acceleration distance of the foot which contributes to reaching a high ball velocity. The ball is hit with the inner instep, i.e. with the inner surface of the centre of the foot. When shooting with the right foot, the centre of contact is usually to the right next to and slightly below the centre of the ball. Thus the ball gets a left spin and takes off more steeply. The take-off angle can be increased by hitting the ball well below its centre in combination with an increased leaning back of the upper body. In respect of fixation of the joints during the follow-through swing of the kicking leg after ball contact the same remarks apply as for the shot with the inside of the foot.

Picture series showing the inner instep shot

5.2.2 Exercise and Game Forms

- **Long Pass**
  Two partners stand facing each other about 20-30 m apart. If the player without the ball runs to the right or left, he receives a long pass with the inner instep from his partner.

- **Stopping a Long Pass**
  Starting position as in the previous exercise. If the ball takes off too low, it can be stopped by an opponent at half the distance and there is an exchange of roles.

- **Goal Shots from a Diagonal Position**
  After dribbling through a goal made of poles erected in a half right or half left position, a shot at goal is taken from about 12 m away with the left or right inner instep. The ball should be shot at the goal from a sharp angle alternately low, medium-high or high in the direction of the rear post.

- **Goal Shot from a Turn**
  After dribbling on the left wing the ball is taken parallel to the goal line at the level of the 16-m-line, and at the level of the penalty shot position a shot at the goal is taken out of a turn using the inner instep.

- **Inner Instep Shots in Standard Situations**
  In free kicks and corners (with/without side spin) the ball is shot at the goal with inner instep shots alternately with and without side spin.

- **Free Play Four-on-two towards a Goal with Goalkeeper**
  While goals scored with inner instep kicks from the right or left wing count double, shots using other techniques are only counted once.

5.3 Outer Instep Shot

Outer instep shot

5.3.1 Application and Technique

Shots with the outer instep of the foot are used diversely in the course of a soccer game. This technique is made use of for short passes as well as for passes over a medium distance and also for shots at goal. As with the inner instep shot, when kicking with the outer instep the ball can be played straight or with side spin. An outer instep shot over a short distance can be an element of surprise for the opponent if the ball is played without backlift in the form of a prekicking swing that can be recognised early. Of necessity the outer instep shot is used by players who can only master a safe pass with the right or left foot: instead of an inner instep shot with the "weak" foot there tends to be an outer instep shot with the "strong" foot. But also players who do not master the full instep shot frequently kick the ball with the outer instep instead. This applies to all those who wish to avoid touching the ground with their toes before ball contact because of a long foot or a lack of shooting technique.

As with the previously mentioned shot forms, with the outer instep shot the standing leg is placed next to the ball. The run-up to the ball is either straight or diagonal. If the ball is to have an arched trajectory it must be hit away from its centre. Before a hard shot there must be a long prekick swinging movement of the kicking leg. In order to hit the ball with the outer instep, the foot must be turned inwards during the swing forwards. The upper body leans slightly forward during the run-up. By the time of the follow-up swing after ball contact the body goes from leaning forwards to leaning backwards.

Picture series showing outer instep shot

5.3.2 Exercise and Game Forms

- Zigzag Passing
  Pairs of players pass each other the ball in zigzag form while running slowly about 10 m apart using the right and left outer instep.

- Pass from Kick-off Spot
  Five players without and two players with balls move in the centre circle. The players with the balls dribble to the kick-off spot and pass the ball to a free partner with an outer instep shot.

- Game Three-on-one in a Marked-off Field
  Playing with one or two contacts, the ball is passed on to the partner alternately using the inside of the foot and the outer instep.

(see photos)

Shots with the inside of the foot and outer instep playing three-on-one

- **Diagonal Pass onto a Second Playing Field**
  In each of two diagonally opposite fields about 15 m apart and 10 m x 10 m in size there are two (three) players of whom one has a ball. After previous eye contact a low or medium-high outer instep shot is made to a partner on the other playing field.

- **Shots at Goal with the Outer Instep**
  About 5-8 players move outside the penalty area. On a call, a player moves towards the goal and shoots, the ball passed by the coach from the side, towards the goal with an outer instep shot. Depending on the type of pass, the shot can be taken after brief dribbling, directly (without and with side spin) and as a drop kick.

- **Free Play Five-on-two in the Penalty Area**
  Every second pass at the latest must be carried out using an outer instep shot. In doing so both short as well as long passes, and wall passes should be played.

- **Start of Play with the Outer Instep**
  Free play three-on-three in a roughly 15 m x 15 m field bordering on the penalty area. A neutral player moves around the penalty area line and receives a short pass with the outer instep from the player currently in possession of the ball. If this succeeds, this player may carry out a shot at goal after a through pass by the neutral player.

5.4 Whole Instep Shot

5. 4. 1 Application and Technique

The shot with the whole instep is considered the technique with which the greatest ball velocity can be achieved. For this reason it is often used for shots, both with low rolling and bouncing balls. Furthermore the whole instep shot is used too for clear kicks or passes over long distances. The whole instep shot is also used, however, to clear the ball away from difficult situations, as well as for goalkicks. In addition, passing on or lofting the ball over an opposing player should be mentioned, in which the technique is used in combination with a less powerful kick. The advantages with regard to kicking power achieved are, however, linked with a number of difficulties: for one thing, it is necessary that the ball is hit exactly in the centre, also, the toes must point towards the ground. Both often create problems for less skilled players. Experienced

Types of Goal Shot

Whole instep shot

players can carry out the whole instep shot with side spin as well. In this case the ball turns, e.g. in a volley shot or drop kick, around its transverse axis and in the falling part of the trajectory it drops down surprisingly quickly. In this way it is possible to beat an inattentive goalkeeper who is off his line. The run-up to the ball is in a straight line and in the direction of the shot. The standing leg is put down next to the ball with the toes pointing in the flight path of the ball. In order to achieve a hard whole instep shot, the kicking leg must be drawn back a long way in preparation. This prekicking movement is completely natural, as the run-up, the swing of the kicking leg and the shot direction are all at one level. The ball should be kicked centrally in the area of the bones in the middle of the foot which represent relatively firm resistance for power transmission. If the ball contact takes place more in the region of the weaker toe bones, the front of the foot is stretched excessively with a risk of injury; see chapter 4.1 "Basic Information on the Goal Shooting Movement". Because of the high velocity of the kicking leg, it is not advisable to carry out the follow-through swing abruptly. A bending of the knee after hitting the ball contributes to controlled braking by the lower leg and foot.

Picture series whole instep shot

5.4.2 Exercise and Game Forms

- **One-on-one Facing the Goal**
  The attacker approaches a defender running backwards, dribbles around him and then from a distance of about 12-16 m shoots at goal with the whole instep.

- **Shooting after a Pursuit**
  The attacker runs towards the goal from a distance of about 30 m and is pursued by a defender. In spite of the challenge the attacker tries to execute a shot at goal with the whole instep.

- **One-on-one after a Through Pass**
  Two players simultaneously take-off after a through pass from the coach at a distance of about 30 m from the goal. The one who gets possession of the ball first executes a whole instep shot at goal while the other person challenges.

- **Shooting after Cross Pass Play**
  Two players approach the goal playing each other cross passes. When the coach calls, the person with the ball becomes the attacker and tries to score a goal with a whole instep shot against the challenge of his team-mate.

- **Shooting with Support of a Back Field Player**
  Free play four-on-four towards a goal. The team in possession of the ball is supported by a back field player and tries to score a goal with a whole instep shot. *Variation:* The back field player may score goals from outside the penalty area.

- Shooting from within and outside the Penalty Area
  Free play four-on-four towards a goal. Shots at goal within the penalty area may only be taken directly or with an initial touch and count once, shots from outside the penalty area with the whole instep count double.

- Shooting under Time Pressure
  Free play four-on-four towards a goal. Following the directions of the coach, after the fifth (sixth) pass at the latest there must be a finishing shot at goal with the whole instep.

5.5 Special Forms

Special form

5.5.1 Application and Technique

The special forms of shooting technique include the hip turning shot, the overhead shot and the volley. These forms are relatively difficult to execute and are only used in rare cases. For this reason they will only be covered briefly. It is characteristic of these types of shot that the ball is usually not controlled first but rather shot directly with the whole instep.

The *hip turning shot* is executed when the ball is to the side of the player at hip level and a shot is to be carried out which is fast and surprising for the opponent. The ball is hit with the outstretched knee after an introductory turn around the body's axis and a wide back-swing of the kicking leg.

Typical playing situations where the *overhead shot* is used are those where there needs to be an immediate clearance or a snap shot at goal with a high flying ball. After a start like a scissors shot, with the body in a horizontal position, the ball is hit above head level.

The *volley* is also a surprise element in the game because the ball is shot first time. This occurs both during a defensive clearance and with a snap shot at goal. The technique is similar to that of the whole instep shot. The difficulty with the volley, however, is to directly take the ball moving towards the player and shoot accurately in the desired direction.

| *Hip turning shot* | *Overhead shot* | *Volley* |

5.5.2 Exercise and Game Forms

a) Hip Turning Shot

- **Hip Turning Shot in Groups of Three**
  Three players stand in a triangle about 10 m apart. A throws the ball to B after a single rebound, B executes a hip turning shot and C catches the ball.

Types of Goal Shot

- **Hip Turning Shot after Ball Control with the Chest**
  One player stands at the penalty area line with his back to the goal. He receives a high thrown or passed ball with his chest, lets it bounce once to the side and executes a hip turning shot at the goal.

- **Soccer Tennis with Hip Turning Shot**
  On a field of about 5 m x 10 m, soccer tennis is played four-on-four. The ball may only be played into the opposite court with a hip turning shot over the approx. 1 m high rope.

b) Overhead Shot
- **Overhead Shot Standing Still**
  After throwing the ball up high – after a single rebound or directly - an overhead shot to a partner without a falling movement is carried out.

- **Overhead Shot after a Straight Throw of the Ball**
  One player stands level with the penalty spot with his back to the goal and kicks a ball thrown frontally from the penalty area line towards the goal after an overhead shot.

- **Overhead Shot after the Ball is Thrown from the Side**
  Exercise as above; this time, however, the throw or pass comes diagonally from the front from the direction of the goal line.

c) Volley
- **Volley after a Backward Pass**
  Two players run behind each other towards the goal, about 2-3 m apart. The player in front with the ball passes the ball back to his partner with the sole of his foot, the partner then executes a volley at the goal.

- **Volley after a Sideways Pass**
  One player dribbles across the side line of the penalty area and passes from the side to a freely running partner. The latter shoots the ball at the goal with a volley.

- **Volley in a Game with Superior Numbers**
  Free play four-on-four with a neutral player towards a goal. The team currently playing with superior numbers is only allowed to shoot at goals with direct shots.

Ball control

6 Ball Control

6.1 Application and Technique

In connection with every passing action where the ball is not immediately moved on, ball control first takes place. Thus the corresponding techniques have a similar significance to the types of shot previously mentioned. Ball control is a necessary prerequisite for orderly teamwork. It should be given appropriate consideration in the training of players at all performance levels, for imperfect mastery of the ball leads to unnecessary loss of possession. High playing speed, close marking and restricted space require particularly secure control of the ball. Thus "stopping" the ball dead is no longer up-to-date: directly after receiving, the ball is moved along and both actions together form a complete movement.

The following illustration provides an overview of the various forms of ball control.

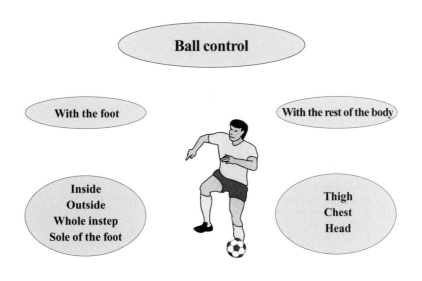

Various forms of ball control

65

As can be seen from this structure, control of the ball occurs mainly with the foot. The other parts of the body are used for receiving and moving high balls. Before the individual forms are described and illustrated, a number of peculiarities about this will be emphasised which are of general significance:

➤ When receiving the ball you should take the pace off the ball.
➤ To do this the particular part of the body first moves towards the ball and then away from it.
➤ During impact the muscles of the surrounding area tense, the other body segments, however, should remain freely movable.
➤ After this the ball must be close to the receiving player so he can carry it forward.

a) Ball Control with the Foot
– Inside

Here three variants are differentiated, the application of which depends on the direction of the passed ball:

1) *Rolling ball:*   The lower leg is bent back diagonally, the knee moved over the ball and the toes are raised slightly.

(see picture series on the next page (above))

2) *Bounced ball:* The ball flying towards the player bounces before him, is pressed to the ground with the inside of the foot, with the lower leg bent to the back, the upper body leans forward.

(see picture series on the next page (centre))

3) *High-flying ball:*   The ball reaches the player at about knee level, the inside of the foot of the receiving leg bent at the knee is moved towards the ball, the upper body remains upright.

(see picture series on the next page (below))

Control of a rolling ball

Control of a bouncing ball

Control of a high-flying ball

– Outside
The same breakdown applies to ball reception with the outside of the foot as to the previously covered inside. Briefly, the most important characteristics are as follows: the leg receiving the ball is moved outwards diagonally in front of the body. At the same time there is a turning outwards along the longitudinal axis of the foot so that the part of the foot concerned comes in contact with the ball. To avoid the ball bouncing away, the toes are lowered slightly. The rounding of the foot arch, extremely necessary turning outwards as well as the unfavourable body position in relation to the ball, means this technique appears more difficult than reception with the inside of the foot.

(see picture series on page 69 (above))

– Whole Instep
With the whole instep of the foot almost exclusively flying balls are received and only rarely bouncing balls. As with the kick, so too with receiving, the ball must touch the middle area of the foot exactly if it is not to bounce away uncontrolled. The faster the ball approaches, the further the foot must be moved towards it with the knee bent. In order to reduce ball velocity the foot must be taken back again briefly before and during ball contact. With this form of ball reception, immediately moving on with the ball is also usually linked with a greater time loss than with the previously mentioned techniques.

(see picture series on page 69 (centre))

– Sole of the Foot
Reception with the sole of the foot is used for low rolling balls and balls which bounce directly in front of the player. The leg is bent at the knee and moved towards the ball. In order that the sole of the foot has ball contact over as great a length as possible, the toes are raised considerably. After the ball is under control, it should be immediately played on with the sole of the foot: either towards the player (better securing of the ball) or more away from him (transition to dribbling). As with reception with the whole instep, this form is also not suited to increasing game speed.

(see picture series on page 69 (below))

b) Ball Control with the Rest of the Body
Under this heading all of the techniques are included where reception with the foot is not possible because of the height of the approaching ball.

Ball control with the outside of the foot

Ball control with the whole instep

Ball control with the sole of the foot

69

- Thigh

The front thigh muscles, which are softer in comparison to the foot surfaces, are well-suited for reducing the velocity of the approaching ball. The thigh moves towards the ball with the knee bent. The platform area should be closer to the torso than to the knee because this is where the ball loses most velocity. After impact the thigh is quickly lowered. After this the ball falls to the ground in front of the player and can be moved on with the foot.

(see picture series on page 71 (above))

- Chest

Because of its size the player's chest provides a suitable surface for ball reception.
Two variants are differentiated:

1) Reception by falling trajectory of the bal: The body is turned frontally to the approaching ball. By pushing the hips forward the upper body is first leaned slightly backwards. Shortly before contact the torso is then moved a little towards the ball with tensed chest muscles. By simultaneously bending at the knees the whole body is lowered in support which reduces the velocity of the ball. As with reception with the thigh the ball is then played on with the foot when it falls to the ground.

(see picture series on page 71 (centre))

2) Reception by rising trajectory of the ball: Here too the player stands opposite the ball in a parallel open foot position. By moving the shoulders forwards the upper body is put in a forward-leaning position in order to thus create resistance to the ball bouncing upwards. When the ball hits the chest the hips are moved back to reduce ball velocity. After contact with the upper body the ball bounces to the ground and is taken over by the foot.

- Head

If ball control with the chest is not possible because of the high trajectory of the ball, and if a direct header seems unsuitable at the moment, the ball is received with the head. This form is difficult because the hard forehead section of the head usually causes the ball to bounce far away. When the ball hits, a rapid bending of the leg joints must take place. During the whole movement the ball must remain in the player's field of vision and it should not bounce off backwards. *The following securing of the ball often only succeeds if an opponent is not directly near the receiving player.*

(see picture series on page 71 (below))

Reception with the thigh

Reception with the chest

Reception with the head

6.2 Exercise and Game Forms

a) Groups of Two without Pressure by Opponents

- **Ball Control with Dribbling**
  A passes the ball to B at various heights, who after every control dribbles briefly then passes back to A.

- **Ball Control before First Ground Contact**
  A passes the ball to B at various heights in an arch, B must control the ball before or on first ground contact.

- **Controlling the Ball and Keeping It in the Air**
  A and B stand about 2-3 m apart facing each other. The ball, juggled in the air, must be played to the partner in such a way that he can alternately control it with his foot, his thigh, his chest or his head.

- **Ball Control after Acceleration**
  A passes the ball to player B standing about 10-15 m away who determines the timing and direction of the pass with a brief acceleration. The ball must be received and moved onwards while running and is then passed back to player A.

b) Several Players, with Pressure by Opponents

Note: Make sure both feet are used; combine receiving with a body feint; after getting control of the ball change direction and/or pace.

- **Ball Control in a Game 1 plus One-on-one plus 1**
  Passer 1 passes the ball to his freely running fellow player. The latter receives the ball in the face of pressure by a defender and passes it off to passer 2 standing opposite him.

- **Ball Control in a Game 1 plus Five-on-five in one Half**
  A passer standing in the centre circle plays passes one after another to five marked forwards. After getting away from the opponent, and controlling the ball, it is either passed on to a fellow attacker, dribbled with a following cross in front of the goal, or the player beats a defender to score.

- **Ball Control in a Game 2 plus Three-on-three in the Penalty Area**
  Crosses are made alternately from the right and left into the penalty area to three marked attackers. After ball control a goal should be scored (point for the attackers) either as an individual action or from team-play. If the defenders gain the ball, they pass it to the opposite passer (point for defenders).

- **Ball Control in a Game 1 plus 2 Times Three-on-three**
  A passer utilises his three attackers from the centre line with varied passes. After getting control of the ball they try to pass it on to one of the three forwards in the penalty area. Here, after first winning the ball under pressure, a goal is scored.

Ball control in game one-on-one

Dribbling

7 Dribbling

7.1 Application and Technique

Although soccer is developing more and more into a fast game with few ball contacts by individuals, without a doubt dribbling is of great importance. Depending on the game situation and tactical intentions, three different forms of dribbling are differentiated (see illustration).

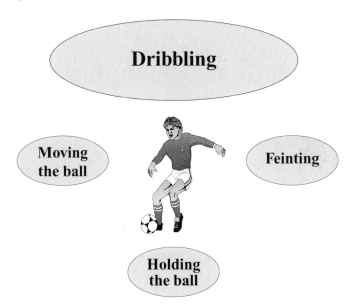

Breakdown of the various forms of dribbling

The term *"moving the ball"* means driving the ball forwards at varying pace. It is used for all kinds of ways of covering space with the ball, such as e.g. starting an attack or bridging the centre field without immediate pressure by a defender. When driving the ball onwards with the whole instep a high running tempo can be reached because of the natural foot and leg posture. When there are changes of direction and tempo, however, other parts of the foot are also used for ball control. In order to keep the ball close, the impulse transmitted through the foot to the ball must be adapted to running speed. Furthermore the player must briefly look up from the ball in order to follow the rest of play.

(see photo on next page above (left))

"Holding the ball" is aimed at controlling the ball without gaining much ground. It is used when the game is to be slowed down for tactical reasons, when no fellow player is standing unmarked at the moment or when no immediate attack action is intended. Finally, *"feinting"* serves to wrong foot and distract the opponent. It is mainly used when in possession of the ball and is aimed at playing away from the approaching defender with appropriate movements. In this form of dribbling the body must always be moved between the opponent and the ball. The shoulder on the side of the standing leg is leaned towards the attacker so that the ball can be controlled with the kicking leg on the other side. If the opponent changes his position, constant adaptation is necessary through corresponding movement of the body and leading of the ball which requires great concentration.

(see photo on next page above (right))

"Feinting" especially serves to dribble successfully in a one-on-one. The possibilities for wrong footing the opponent with deceptive movements are diverse, are often varied. Here we will briefly cover a few common forms:

a) *"Feint to the right, passing on the left"*. The person with the ball dribbles directly towards the defender. With a lunge to the right he feints a move past the opponent on this side, then, however, he uses the left outer instep to move the ball past the defender.

(see picture series on next page (centre))

b) *"Step over"*. Once again both players move towards each other. As a feint the attacker moves his right foot as if stepping over the ball kept close to his body. If the defender also shifts his weight to this side, the attacker races past him with an acceleration to the left.

(see picture series on next page (below))

"Moving the ball"

"Holding the ball"

"Feint to the right, passing on the left"

"Step over"

c) *"Feint shot"*. The attacking player plays the ball e.g. as a winger. His opponent is diagonally opposite him and expects a form of a pass or a centre. The person with the ball feints this with a pronounced swinging back movement of the kicking leg. The defender then moves his outer foot for the purpose of blocking the ball. Now the attacker quickly stops the shooting movement and with the inside of his foot takes the ball in front of the defender towards the centre.

(see picture series on following page (above))

d) *"Kick on to the left, race past on the right"*. The attacker dribbles towards a defender at high speed. Before the defender can make a move, the forward slips the ball with the instep past him to the left, low and without swinging back obviously. He then runs around the defender to the right with an accelerated dash and gets the ball under control again as quickly as possible.

(see picture series on following page (centre))

c) *"Nutmeg"*. With this trick, which is extremely risky from the point of view of the person with the ball, an attempt is made with deceptive movements to get the opponent to stand with his legs apart. Once this is achieved, in a surprise move the ball is kicked low between his legs using the inside of the foot. After a rapid acceleration past the defender the ball is taken up again.

(see picture series on following page (below))

7.2 Technique Analysis

Experimental analyses show that there are different power conditions present in a change of direction in all three dimensions than there are when dribbling straight ahead. Steeper rises in power and a longer supporting time characterise a diversion from the direction of movement. In order to quickly and successfully carry out deceptive movements, the player's moving apparatus must meet special demands. In addition to the leg extensor muscles which work with a giving and overcoming effect, the inner thigh and lower leg muscles must also be sufficiently strong. As well as this the stabilising ligaments of the upper ankle and knee joints contribute in no small way to the absorption of horizontal and vertical forces. In training, strengthening of muscles involved in deceptive movements can be achieved with runs with changes of direction, lunges and gymnastic exercises. To make possible the necessary transmission of forces from the ground to the body, the boots must be adapted to ground conditions e.g. with appropriate studs.

"Feint shot"

"Kick forward on the left, race past on the right"

"Nutmeg"

Soccer Technique

7.3 Exercise and Game Forms

a) "Moving the ball"
- **Varied Dribbling**

  The player carries out medium-fast dribbling without pressure. At a shout or signal from the coach, running speed or direction are changed as quickly as possible while keeping the ball under control.

- **Pursuit Dribbling**

  After a simultaneous start from the centre line two players carry out slalom dribbling around five flag sticks. They should reach the penalty area line as quickly as possible and then take a shot at goal. *Variation:* After about 5 m head start the dribblers are pursued by a defender who tries to stop the shot at goal.

- **Stopping a Dribble**

  On a field of about 15 m x 15 m five players with the ball under control try to fend off five other players without the ball. When the ball is successfully taken, roles are swapped.

b) "Holding the Ball"
- **Winning the Ball**

  On a playing field of about 10 m x 10 m five players shield the ball. Five other players without a ball attack and try to win the ball and take it away to an equally large zone opposite.

  Variation: If a player loses the ball he is allowed to run after it and get it back into his half.

- **Securing Ball Position**

  Two players dribble holding the ball in the centre circle in a one-on-one. The person with the ball must play it to a fellow player, who races from the penalty area line, while he is outside the centre circle. After a successful pass, an attack takes place (two-on-one) on the goal, which is completed by the person previously holding the ball taking a shot at goal.

- **Shooting off the Ball**

  On a playing field about 20 m x 20 m five players carry out a ball holding dribble. Five other players have the task of playing each other the ball in such a way that a targeted shot against the ball of a ball holding player is possible. When a "shoot-off" is successful, there is a change of roles.

c) "Deception and Feinting"

- One-on-one in a Square

  A player stands at each corner of a square with sides about 10 m in length. In this area one-on-one is played. On getting possession of the ball each participant has the task of passing it to a previously named corner player after dribbling with deception. After a successful action, positions are swapped.

- Three Times One-on-one Using three Small Goals

  The players in possession of the ball have the task of feigning an attack on one of the three approx. 2 m wide goals. If after a successful feint they get around the defender, they must dribble through one of the small goals. Afterwards the two players swap roles.

- Four-on-six on a Marked-off Field

  On an approx. 20 m by 20 m playing-field each team section tries to keep the ball among their own ranks as long as possible: the players of the group of four can only play-off after dribbling past their opposite numbers with previous deception. The players of the group of six must take the ball further after two (three) contacts at the most.

8 Heading

Heading at goal

8.1 Application and Technique

In today's soccer game an effort is made to keep the ball mainly low and at a height where it can be reached with the foot. Nevertheless there are a number of situations in which it is advisable to vary from this guideline. These include among others the goalkeeper's kick, the clearance by the defender, the through pass of the midfield player, or the cross from the right or left wing. In dead ball situations such as the free kick, the corner or throw-in, the ball usually flies high towards fellow players. In order to receive the ball after such a pass and knock it in a particular direction, the technique of heading must be mastered. It is extremely diverse as the table on the following page shows.

Heading

Header

While standing

While running

While jumping

Body position: frontal or sideways
Ball flight direction: forwards, sideways or backwards
Jump-off: One- or two-legged

Breakdown of various forms of heading

Depending on the height of the ball and tactical intentions, the header is done while standing, running or jumping. In doing so you stand either frontally or sideways to the ball. The direction the ball flies off to is either straight ahead, to the side or to the back, whereby the trajectory can be upwards, horizontal or downwards. The jump-off for a header is either one- or two-legged.

As the breakdown above shows, heading technique is characterised by diverse variations. The following notes contain basic information on the techniques of heading without going into the individual forms in detail. After this the results of technique and load analyses are included.

When executing a header, not only the movement of the head must be considered, but also of the whole body. If the ball is to be headed with a hard and well-placed strike, it is necessary, as with the shot with the foot, to take a drawn back swing in preparation. This pretenses the muscles involved and lengthens the acceleration path of the head. Before this the trajectory of the approaching ball should be followed as far as possible in order to be aware of potential diversions (spin, wind, opponent) and to react to them. The player should move actively towards the ball and not let it "passively" reach him. For anatomical reasons the forehead is the best contact surface for the ball. Shortly before and during the header the neck and torso muscles in particular must be tensed in order to create firm resistance. If the header is in combination with a one-on-one, additionally attention must be given to use of the arm and shoulder muscles. In this way the body of the player has additional stability which is necessary for the execution of a controlled header. The following picture series show the main forms of the various heading techniques.

Header while standing, stepping and jumping
(upper body frontal to the ball)

Header while jumping (upper body sideways to the ball)

Header while jumping with change of direction

Leaping header

8.2 Technique Analysis

In videographic motion analyses two forms were studied: the header while standing and while jumping. In addition to other factors, velocity of certain parts of the body in the course of movement were evaluated. It became evident that the horizontal velocity of the shoulders and the head are constantly increased and drop shortly before contact. The player thus moved quickly towards the ball and braked with the shoulders and head directly before contact. The velocity of the hips was initially increased slightly, then dropped because of the pronounced forward movement of the parts of the body above it. It does not, however, show any negative values as the centre of gravity of the player's body moved more quickly towards the ball than the hips. These analyses show, briefly summarised, a number of results with a close relationship to practical situations.

- Header while standing:
➤ The stride position should be given preference to the parallel closed leg position; it allows longer acceleration distances and makes it easier to achieve higher velocities of the individual parts of the body.
➤ The greater the velocities of hips, shoulders and head, both at the beginning of the movement and on ball contact, the greater the take-off velocity of the ball is as well.
➤ A greater horizontal acceleration distance of the body's centre of gravity, i.e. "active" movement towards the ball, also leads to high velocities of the ball at take-off.

- Header while jumping up:
➤ With relation to the starting and ending velocities of the hips, shoulders and head, the same results were recorded as with heading while standing.
➤ The take-off velocity of the ball was higher the more the ball flew horizontally in the direction of the goal after contact.
➤ The higher the players jumped when heading, the lower was the speed of the ball at take-off.

The above results with regard to head velocity were confirmed and made more precise in a further study. Here the participants wore two acceleration metres on their heads. It became evident that experienced players negatively accelerate their head directly before ball contact by stiffening their neck muscles, i.e. they brake. Less skilled players, on the other hand, still show positive acceleration values as a result of too little use of the back and neck muscles shortly before ball contact, which often leads to a backward rotation of the head afterwards.

8.3 Load Analysis

After reading through the literature on this subject it can be concluded that to date there has been no analysis which has proved a connection between heading and later damage to health. A study on frequency showed that a professional soccer player executes more than 5000 heading actions in the course of fifteen years in competitive games. Acute injuries to the head, however, occur only rarely during heading itself; they result mainly from external influences such as collision or unexpected shooting. Although to date there is no final evidence, the risk of long-term damage arising as a result of heading cannot be excluded. The effect of forces on the head depend on three factors:

a) *The mechanical properties of the ball*; its circumference, mass, air pressure and material represent "external" conditions.

b) *The physique characteristics of the player;* players with low weight are exposed to greater forces in relation to body mass. This statement is especially significant in the youth area, where special emphasis should be put on ball material suitable for the age-group.

c) *The technique when heading;* the externally visible movement process and the non-visible use of various muscle groups also contributes to the degree that forces have an effect.

To date there are uncertainties in the evaluation of influences of technique on the dangers of possible head injuries. On the one hand, in the case of experienced players, a major danger is suspected because of their "good" technique as major acceleration of the head. On the other hand it is recommended in order to improve technique, to use lighter footballs, to execute as few heading actions as possible (especially after "hard" shots from a close distance), in order to reduce the danger of injury to the head. In order to obtain reliable information on this problem it is certain that further research is needed.

8.4 Exercise and Game Forms

- **Start towards the Ball**
  A player only heads back the ball thrown by a partner if he is moving at a run in the direction of the ball flying towards him.

- **Passing on the Ball**
  Five players jog on a 10 m x 10 m sized field and have the task of passing on the thrown ball to one of the other players with their heads.

- **Getting away from the Opponent**
  A player is closely covered by a defender and receives a throw for a header only after getting away from the opponent.

- **Handball Header**
  Members of team A throw the ball to each other according to the rules of handball and try to get a goal with a header when thrown the ball. Team B disrupts the teamwork and is allowed to catch the ball outside the goal area and to head it away within the goal area.

- **Handball Header Soccer Game**
  Team A tries to get a header goal after being thrown the ball whereby the opponents defend as in handball. If team B has the ball, a free soccer game takes place in the direction of the centre line, whereby the opponents defend as soccer players.

- **Calling for a High Pass**
  Five players move between the 11-metre-spot and the penalty area line at a jog. By taking off towards the goal a player signals a winger to give him a high cross that is headed towards the goal.

- **Variable Heading Game**
  In the penalty area there are three attackers and two defenders. After a high cross from a winger the attackers try to score a direct headed goal or to pass the ball on with the head and from the free combination game to take a shot at goal.

- **Header and Counter Play**
  Free play 2 plus three-on-three in half a pitch. Team A is allowed to involve the two neutral players when in possession of the ball and to score headed goals. Team B, when in possession of the ball, tries with the support of the two neutral players to dribble through an opposite goal at the level of the centre line.

8.5 Heading Training with the Pendulum

To improve heading technique, often additional training with a heading pendulum is recommended. This form offers the following advantages among others: an effective exercise sequence, high intensity, the possibility of individual and group training, doing without a thrower or winger, speed of ball velocity (from resting to quickly approaching through the air), an automatisation of the motion sequence under constant conditions, the execution of almost all variations of heading and achieving a combined training effect of technique and strength.

With the heading pendulum, however, there are a number of disadvantages: getting accustomed to the device, adjusting to unnatural trajectories of the ball (the ball moves downwards towards the player), doing without an arched trajectory of the ball as in crosses with spin, a ball that moves to the player with growing speed as a result of the pendulum whereas a thrown or crossed ball moves uniformly or usually slows down with increasing flight duration.

Without a doubt the header pendulum is a useful aid. A positive training effect can be expected in particular with youths. If the device is used too often, however, adaptation problems to freely played balls can be expected for the reasons mentioned.

Throw-in

9 Throw-in

9.1 Application and Technique

If in the course of the game the ball crosses the sideline, the game is continued by means of a throw-in. To secure ball possession the throw-in is usually done over a short or medium distance to a fellow player in a position to receive it. In some cases, however, a throw-in of the ball over a longer distance is recommended. Thus a long throw-in e.g. into one's own half, or in the centre circle, can be as effective as a cross. Because with a throw-in there is no direct offside situation, sometimes it is possible as a surprise tactic to get behind the opposite defence in this way. Close to the goal, a long throw-in can even have the effect of a free-kick or a corner, which provides opportunities for scoring. From this it becomes clear that with varied use of the throw-in, advantages in a practical sense result which are all too frequently unused. With regard to its execution the throw-in can be broken down as follows.

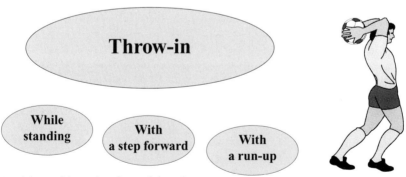

Breakdown of the various forms of throw-in

When standing, usually a parallel foot position is assumed whereas with a step the throwing of the ball is done in a stride position. When doing a throw-in after a run-up, both legs are also in a stride position, sometimes in the course of the throw the back foot is brought forward.

Soccer coaching books contain few recommendations on the execution of this movement

Soccer Technique

The individual execution of the movements of a throw-in are subject to certain restrictions due to the laws of the game. The player must be behind the sideline with both feet, must face the playing field, must touch the ground with both feet when throwing and must continuously hold the ball with both hands over his head. The following picture series show the motion sequence of the throw-in when standing and with a run-up.

Throw-in while standing

Throw-in with a run-up

especially for the difficult long throw-in. Usually, as with almost all soccer techniques, there is just a general description. Because of a lack of knowledge, usually emphasis of the main characteristics which could lead to concrete training information is done without. There is, however, concrete data on the throw-in which will now be covered more closely.

9.2 Technique Analysis

In the course of an experimental study soccer players had the task of executing throw-ins while standing and with a run-up in a competition-like situation. The movements were recorded with a special video camera and afterwards evaluated with the help of a computer. Here briefly are the main results:

➤ On average the players achieved greater distances after throw-ins with a run-up than when standing (20.20 m as opposed to 23.70 m).

➤ The individual improvements in distance with throw-ins after a run-up, as opposed to throw-ins while standing, were between 1.5 m and 13 m.

➤ The externally visible motion sequence, described by the leg and torso angle, were extremely varied from player to player and showed no relationship to the distance.

➤ When throwing-in while standing the following factors aid distance: a great hip velocity in the backward swing-back position and a high hand and ball velocity at the throw-in. A short throw-in time should be attempted while maintaining an equally long acceleration distance of the ball.

➤ When throwing with a run-up the following factors aid distance: high run-up velocity, high hand and ball velocities at the throw, as well as high final acceleration of the ball briefly before the throw. Both are favoured by a longer acceleration distance of the ball and a longer throwing time, whereby a low, backward lowering of the ball is necessary when swinging back.

The take-off velocity of the ball can be considered as the factor which most greatly influences the distance of the throw. In addition, however, also throwing height and above all the angle of take-off of the ball are decisive. A comparison showed that all players threw the ball an average 10° too low in relation to the achievable optimum. This led to losses in distance of more than 5 m. Comments on movement intended to improve distance should be less related to the particular body posture ("bend at the knees more", "arch yourself more"), but rather more to the results mentioned.

9.3 Exercise and Game Forms

- **Individual Competition**
  In groups of 4-6 players each tries, first with throw-ins while standing and then with throw-ins after a run-up, to achieve a maximum throwing distance. Fellow players mark the distance and play the balls back.

- **Driving Ball Game**
  With throw-ins two players try to force the partner as far as possible over a target line. If a player intercepts the ball, he may move forward two steps.

- **Throw-in Game**
  Player A executes a long throw-in towards a freely running fellow player B who then gets the ball under control and dribbles towards the position of player A. The ball throw should be alternately low and steep.

- **Game One-on-one after a Long Throw-in**
  The forward gets away from his opponent and tries to score a goal either directly with a header or shot, or after previously receiving the ball.

- **Game Two (3)-on-two (3) after a Long Throw-in**
  The attacking players try to score a goal through headers, direct shots, or second balls not cleared far enough. The thrower joins the game and supports the attack.

- **Game Two (3)-on-two (3) after a Long Throw-in Followed by a Counterattack.**
  Game form as above, but when the defenders are in possession of the ball they try to reach the centre line with a counterattack. The thrower becomes the neutral player and supports either the attackers in a fast goal action or the defenders starting a counterattack, depending on who is in possession of the ball.

10 Goalkeeping

Safe interception of the ball

10.1 Application and Technique

Because of his special function the techniques of the goalkeeper vary considerably to those of the field players. To make his job easier, the goalkeeper is the only member of the team who is allowed to play the ball with his hands as well. His main task is to prevent goals by the opposition. But also in the build-up of the game, the introduction of an attack by his own team, the goalkeeper has a decisive role. The main techniques of the goalkeeper in the two areas named can be seen on the following page.

Soccer Technique

Defence

Catch, roll away, dive, palm, punch, saving with the feet

Goalkeeper technique

Game build-up

Roll, throw, hit, goal kick

Breakdown of the techniques of the goalkeeper

As well as mastering these techniques the goalkeeper's game is linked with tactical tasks. His favourable location gives the goalkeeper a good overview of the whole playing field. He is thus in a position to support his fellow players. This includes e.g. directing the defenders to make a "wall" to defend a free kick.

The breakdown shown here includes the techniques which the goalkeeper carries out with the ball. Here, however, his movements without the ball and towards the ball should not be neglected. These include for one thing the ready position which is taken up before every action. Through slight bending at the foot, knee and hip joints the body's centre of gravity is lowered and the torso brought into a forward-leaning position. The body weight is shifted to over the toes. In connection with a roughly hip wide position of the feet a ready position is thus taken up which creates favourable prerequisites for successful jumping, rolling away or diving.

The body position described is characterised by major activity of the leg and torso muscles. The muscle tension thus created favours rapid execution of movements. The goalkeeper also achieves this effect when he moves a few steps from the goal line towards the playing field to defend a shot. Here from a parallel position of the feet, both a strong jumping position is in place as well as achieving a "shortening of the angle".

(see picture series on page 98 (two above))

If, however, the ball is not close to the goal, the goalkeeper should be involved in loosening and relaxing exercises. Such gymnastics, also in combination with slow running, contribute both to physical and also mental relaxation. In low temperatures this type of movement also prevents the body from cooling down.

The other techniques of the goalkeeper can be described briefly as follows:

- Catching:
When straight low shots come, take up a relatively narrow foot position; stand behind the ball and take it with funnel-formed opened hands and secure it against the body.

(see picture series on next page (centre))

With low shots from the side, or balls that bounce up beforehand, shift your weight to the bent standing leg and kneel down with the other leg.

(see picture series on next page (below))

In the case of frontal goal shots at hip level or above head level the body is again behind the ball, which is caught with both hands with fingers spread out and then held close to the chest.

(see photo series on page 99 (above and centre))

- Rolling away:
When low shots come from the side the body is lowered by bending the knees; the outside of the foot, lower leg, thigh, torso and arm touch the ground one after the other; the ball is taken up with one hand from behind and then with the other from above.

(see photo series on page 99 (below))

Running out with a starting stride

Catching the ball after straight low shots

Catching the ball after low shots from the side

Catching the ball at chest level

Catching the ball at head level

Rolling away in the case of a low shot from the side

Rolling away after Low Shots from the Side
- *Diving:*

After high shots at goal from the side there is a jump with the ball caught with both hands with head and arms stretched; on landing afterwards the parts of the body involved should touch the ground one after the other to cushion the impact.

(see picture series on next page (above))

- *Palming:*

In the case of high shots at goal from the side which do not allow catching with both hands while jumping, the ball is tipped over the goal with one or both hands.

(see picture series on next page (centre))

- *Punching:*

Mostly in the case of crosses, in tight situations or with wet balls, the goalkeeper punches after running out with a jump; both hands are clenched into fists and with quick stretching at the elbow they strike the ball in another direction if possible.

(see picture series on next page (below))

- *Saving with the Feet:*

If a forward tries to push the ball past the goalkeeper or to outplay him, the goalkeeper uses his feet; it is similar to the sliding tackle of the defenders, whereby the briefly unprotected ball is shot away while falling.

(see picture series on page 102 (above))

Another form of saving with the feet is the sideways straddle towards the ball in the case of low shots which for example come from a short distance often with an element of surprise and therefore do not allow catching or rolling away.

- *Game Build-up:*

Depending on tactical intentions, the goalkeeper starts a counterattack in the following way: after a save he distributes the ball through rolling, throwing or kicking the ball away.

(see picture series on page 102 (centre))

Diving

Palming

Punching

Saving with the feet

Rolling, throwing, clearance-kicking

10.2 Technique Analysis

When assessing the performance of a goalkeeper it must be noted that on the one hand the movement sequence itself, and on the other hand the recognising and assessing of the situation, form a unit. In experiments it is difficult to consider simultaneously both these aspects. Therefore to date either only studies of movement sequence have been carried out or in the area of anticipation, perception, or reaction and decision behaviour. Here now briefly results on the technique of diving towards the ball are given.

Goalkeeping

In the case of well-placed shots, after recognising as early as possible direction, height and velocity of the approaching ball, the goalkeeper must quickly execute diving movements. At a ball height of 1.5 m, the diving movements of goalkeepers of a high standard vary from those of lower standard in the following way:

➤ In the course of the take-off, the body's centre of gravity is lowered in preparation.
➤ This is accompanied by a major bending movement at the knees and hips of both legs.
➤ The total duration of the jump-off – until leaving the ground – is longer.
➤ In this way the good goalkeepers manage to achieve a greater take-off velocity.
➤ With the better goalkeepers the horizontal (sideways) component of take-off velocity of the centre of gravity of the body is comparatively greater, the vertical (upwards) component, however, smaller.
➤ Thus the better goalkeepers dive "straighter" and reach the ball after a shorter leaping phase whereas the poorer goalkeepers dive more "steeply" and catch the ball only after a longer leaping phase.

Diving goalkeeper

103

10.3 Exercise and Game Forms

a) Individual Training of the Goalkeeper

Training emphasis: Catching, rolling away, diving.

- **Rolling away from Various Positions**
  The goalkeeper sits on the ground with legs outstretched. He must catch balls shot to him at a low height from both sides by rolling sideways with outstretched arms.
  Variation: Starting positions of the goalkeeper are kneeling and crouching.

- **Catching Bouncing Balls**
  The goalkeeper crouches and alternately catches low balls and throws as bouncing balls by rolling or diving.

- **Diving into the Other Goal Corner**
  The goalkeeper stands at the right goalpost and must reach balls shot low into the left half of the goal by diving.

- **Catching the Ball before Ground Contact**
  The goalkeeper stands in the middle of a 10 m x 10 m field and must catch balls from outside before touching the ground by rolling away or diving.
  Variation: The square is now divided into equally large rectangles in which the balls to be caught are played alternately.

- **Catching Balls Flying from both Sides**
  The goalkeeper catches low or medium-high balls, which are alternately passed to him from in front of and behind a goal made of flag sticks.

Training emphasis: Punching, palming.

- **Long Punching**
  High centre crosses alternately from both sides, whereby the goalkeeper punches the ball far away from the goal when running off his line.

- **Targeted Punching**
  Exercise as before, but now the goalkeeper must punch the ball as accurately as possible to a fellow player who is running into space.

- **Palming the Ball while Running Backwards**
  The goalkeeper stands about 5 m in front of the goal and must palm balls thrown in an arch with a backward movement over the cross bar.

- **Running out in a One-on-one**
  An attacker dribbling towards the goal tries to round the goalkeeper; he tries to prevent a successful goal by running out with hand or foot defence.

b) Team Training with the Goalkeeper
  Training emphasis: Use defence techniques appropriate to the situation, start game build-up.

- **Shots at Goal from Right, Left and Centre**
  Two players are each located on the right wing, the 16-m-line and the left wing. Alternately there are high crosses from the right, shots at goal from the penalty area line and high crosses from the left. To defend the ball the goalkeeper uses the appropriate techniques in each case.

- **Defence against Heading Players**
  Alternately there are crosses from both sides in the 5 m area. Three attackers try to score goals with headers. The goalkeeper tries to catch the balls, punch them or tip them over the bar.

- **Defence of Crosses with Following Action**
  Exercise as before, now the attackers also have the possibility of directing the crosses to fellow players positioned in the back area. These try to overcome the goalkeeper with shots from distance.

- **Defence with Restricted Vision**
  There are alternating shots from about 16-20 m away from half right, the centre and the left. In the penalty area four attackers constantly move backwards and forwards in order to obscure the vision of the goalkeeper. The goalkeeper must catch the balls, punch or palm them, whereby the attackers go after balls not hit far enough away and shoot.

- **Coordination of Goalkeeping and Defence Action**
  Crosses in front of the goal are made alternately from the left and right side. In the penalty area there are four attackers who try to score and three defenders who fulfil defence tasks in co-operation with the goalkeeper.

- **Introduction of a Counterattack**

  Exercise as before, but now the goalkeeper has the task of preparing a counterattack on the flag stick goal at the level of the centre line through accurate punching, rolling or throwing the ball to a fellow player standing free outside the penalty area.

Shot at goal by a young player

II SOCCER TACTICS

All actions in a soccer game must be directed at one objective. This objective, the success of the team, can only be achieved through the co-operation of all players. For this purpose the activities of the individual players must be co-ordinated and there must be appropriate tactics. *The term "tactics" in a soccer game is understood as planned action with the objective of achieving the best possible result under the given conditions.* In all teams it is obvious that successful tactics depend on both individual and combined playing. From this results the following breakdown.

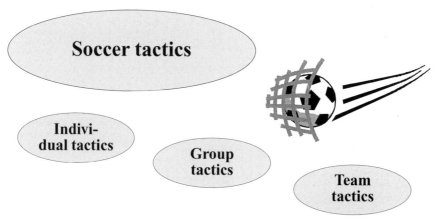

Soccer tactics

The objective of the game of soccer is to score goals and prevent the opponent from doing so. Thus tactics must be divided according to the main tasks the players, the group or the whole team are pursuing in a certain situation. In this connection one speaks of

– attack tactics and
– defence tactics.

These aspects will be covered more closely whereby differences between the particular tactics and appropriate exercise and game forms will be named.

1 Individual Tactics

Individual tactics involves measures which individual players use in certain situations. These measures have significance over and above the individual action both for a group and the whole team. They affect the goalkeeper, the sweeper, the defence, midfield and attack players.

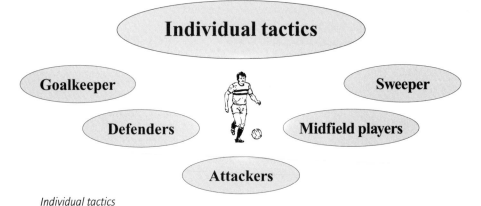

Individual tactics

1.1 Goalkeeper

Goalkeeper punching

Individual Tactics

1.1.1 Tactical Tasks

The most important tactical tasks of the goalkeeper can be seen in the following table.

TACTICS OF THE GOALKEEPER	
Attack tactics	Defence tactics
– Introduction of an attack	– Instructions to the defenders – Positional play in situations: • Shots from various distances • Standard situations • (Free kick, corner kick, penalty kick, throw-in) • Crosses • One-on-one situations

Thanks to his favourable position the goalkeeper can see the whole pitch and can take on responsible tasks. With a goalkick, clearancekick or throw or a palmed ball ball the goalkeeper carries out the first steps to start an attack. This action is significant for the tactics of the attacking game, even though the main tasks of the goalkeeper are of course in defence.

When "directing" the defence the attention of the players must be drawn to attacks of the opponent with loud calling. The positional play of the goalkeeper is a major prerequisite for execution of successful defence. In general the goalkeeper should stand on the bisector of the angle of the ball and both goalposts. The only time this should be varied from is in the case of crosses (crosses, corner kicks) and free kicks with building a wall.

The distance from the goal line must be chosen in such a way that a "shortening of the angle" is exploited without at the same time allowing a chipped shot.

1.1.2 Exercise and Game Forms

Game situation

Emphasis: Fast, situational reaction.

- **Game four-on-four towards two goals open on both sides**

The attackers can score goals from both goal sides from free play. The goalkeeper must quickly adapt to the attack situation in each case.

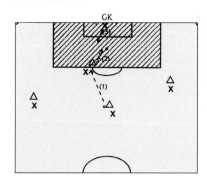

Game situation

Emphasis: Running out of the goal or defence on the line.

- **Game four-on-four with two goals with game build-up on the wing**

The team in possession of the ball can only score a goal when the attack occurs via a high pass from the wing. Then the goalkeeper must quickly decide whether running out (catching, punching) or staying in the goal (defence on the line) is more advisable.

Emphasis: Shorten the angle, foot defence, defence against dribbling.

- **Game four-on-four with one goal and goalkeeper playing out**

Free play four-on-four between the centre line and the penalty area line. A player of the team in possession of the ball tries to penetrate into the penalty area with the ball. The forward may only score a goal after he has beaten the goalkeeper coming off his line.

Game situation

1.2 Sweeper

1.2.1 Tactical Tasks

The most important tactical tasks of the sweeper can be seen in the table below.

In almost all tactical systems a sweeper is active in the area between the goalkeeper and the defenders. In the case of ball possession he starts the attack with a pass. As a "free man" the sweeper is released from direct covering duties and is also responsible with the others for the organisation of defence activity. In doing so he secures the area in front of his own goal with skilled positional playing. If a defender is outplayed, the sweeper must intervene and try to separate the opponent from the ball. Because this usually happens directly close to the goal, the

Sweeper

sweeper's defence actions must be technically flawless with a view to avoiding a free kick or penalty kick. The position of the sweeper must always be filled by an experienced, responsible and technically and tactically skilled player.

TACTICS OF THE SWEEPER	
Attack tactics	**Defence tactics**
– Introduction of an attack	– Organisation of defence
	– Securing of the area in front of the goal
	– Intercepting an opposing attacker

1.2 .2 Exercise and Game Forms

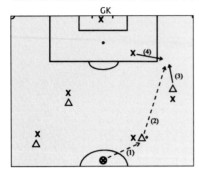

Game situation

Emphasis: Close passing routes, intercept flying balls.

- **Interception of through passes**

Free play 1 (passer) plus 3 against 1 (sweeper) plus 3 towards a goal. The passer tries to make use of a fellow player with through passes, high and long passes or a wall pass. The sweeper's task involves recognising these passes, closing the passing route or intercepting the flying balls.

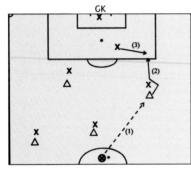

Game situation

Emphasis: Strengthening defence.

- **Supporting man coverage**

Game situation as above. Now the sweeper must step in when a defender of his team is outplayed by a forward and moves towards the goal. In doing so the sweeper must always orient his playing position to the current position of the ball.

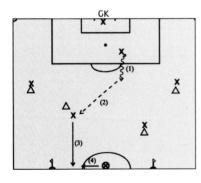

Game situation

Emphasis: Game build-up.

- **Introduction of an attack**

Game situation as above, now team A (with passer) plays towards the normal goal, and team B (with sweeper) plays towards a 20 m wide counter goal at the centre line. If team B has gained the ball, the sweeper prepares a counterattack. Scoring: goal success for team A: one point, dribbling through the counter goal by a forward from team B: one point, the same by the sweeper: two points.

1.3 Defenders

1.3.1 Tactical Tasks

The most important tactical duties of the defence players are listed in the table below.

Together with the goalkeeper and the sweeper the defence players are the core of defence. If a defender has possession of the ball he starts an attack by clearing the ball or dribbling forward into the opposite half.

Defence player

The main field of duties is, however, defence. Through an appropriate position with regard to ball and opponent the defence player disrupts ball control, passing, dribbling, goal shooting or headers of the attackers. In doing so the defender makes use of the techniques mentioned in the previous chapter where one-on-ones are used taking into consideration fair play.

TACTICS OF THE DEFENDERS	
Attack tactics	**Defence tactics**

– Introduction of an attack	– Disruption of the opponent in the following actions:
	    • Ball control
	    • Passing
	    • Dribbling
	    • Goal shooting
	    • Heading

1.3 2 Exercise and Game Forms

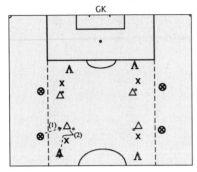

Game situation

Emphasis: Man marking, defence against dribbling.

- **4 times 1 plus one-on-one towards four goals**

At each corner of a field there is a pair of players for a one-on-one as well as a neutral passer and a player who forms a goal by straddling his legs. The defender must stop the co-operation between the passer and the attacker as well as the individual actions of the attacker in order to prevent a shot through the goal formed by the fellow player.

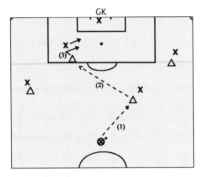

Game situation

Emphasis: Man marking, shield off the path to the goal.

- **Defence of goal shots**

Free play 1 plus four-on-four towards a goal with goalkeeper. There is a fixed ordering of player pairs. The defender must closely mark his opponent, closing him down and not letting him play the ball.

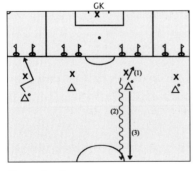

Game situation

Emphasis: Man marking, defence against dribbling, introduction of a counterattack.

- **4 times one-on-one with counterattack**

Four attackers with a ball each try to execute low shots through 2 m wide stick goals despite marking by four defenders. The defence players defend their goal with skilled positional playing and try to get the ball in one-on-ones. If this is successful the defender dribbles, which the attacker must tackle before it reaches the centre line.

1.4 Midfield Players

1.4.1 Tactical Tasks

The tactical duties which must be fulfilled by the midfield players can be seen in the table below.

The range of requirements of midfield players is extremely diverse. Primarily they have the duty of carrying out the planned team tactics (holding the ball, making the game fast, introducing counters).

Midfield player

In the midfield the important switching from defence to attack and vice versa takes place on which game success depends to a major degree. In the attack midfield players must use the forward line, make themselves available for clearances in the rear area and also shoot at goal. Despite the large amount of (intensive running) attack tactical duties, the defence tactical duties must not be neglected. Here the opponent's room to manouevre must be restricted (closing down space), the player with the ball must be harried, and the freely running opponents covered. All these actions require a high degree of fitness and technical and tactical ability by midfield players.

TACTICS OF THE MIDFIELD PLAYERS	
Attack tactics	**Defence tactics**
– Introduction of an attack	– Restriction of the opponent's room to move
– Bridging the midfield	– Harrying of player with the ball
– Feeding the forward line	– Covering freely running players
– Availability at the back	
– Shots at goal	

1.4.2 Exercise and Game Forms

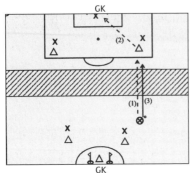

Game situation

Emphasis: Long pass to the forwards.

- **Long pass across a centre zone**

Free play of 1 (midfield player) and 2 times two-on-two towards two goals with goal-keepers. The midfield player supports the team which has the ball at the time. If he is in possession of the ball he carries out a high and long pass over a free central zone, approx. 10-15 m wide, to an attacker on the other side who makes himself available. After this the midfield player moves up and uses one of the two forwards with the intention of scoring a goal.

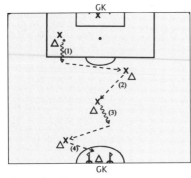

Game situation

Emphasis: Increase game speed.

- **Change between free play and play with two touches**

Free play four-on-four towards two goals with goalkeepers. In order to increase game speed and quickly bridge the space to the opposing goal every second action may only involve play with two touches (control and pass). The player used in between can touch the ball as often as he wants (e.g. in dribbling).

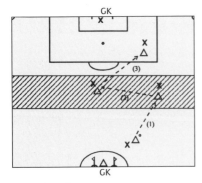

Game situation

Emphasis: Fast bridging of the centre field.

- **Direct play in the centre zone**

Free play four-on-four towards two goals with goalkeepers. On the way to the opponent's goal the ball must be played through a 10-15m wide midfield zone. In this area the players are only allowed to directly play the ball onwards. In the game build-up before and during combining behind the midfield as many ball contacts are allowed.

116

1.5 Attacking Players

1.5.1 Tactical Tasks

Forward

The tactical duties of the attack players can be seen in the table below.

The main tactical task of the attack players consists of setting up and scoring goals. This can occur either through individual actions or in co-operation with the other attacking players.

Through frequent changing of position the attack player contributes to unsettling the opposing defence which can result in situations dangerous to the goal. These include, among others, moving off to the wing, changing sides, and falling back into the midfield. The free areas created in this way can be used by fellow players. The defence tactical duties of the attacker include disrupting the opponents in building up their game and in "following on" in the case of an offensive push by the opposing player.

TACTICS OF THE ATTACKING PLAYERS	
Attack tactics	**Defence tactics**

– Execution of individual actions in front of the opponent's goal
– Actions together with the other attack players:
    • Combination play
    • Change of position
	– Disruption of the opponent's game build-up
	– Covering of offensive opponents

1.5.2 Exercise and Game Forms

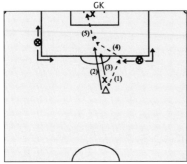

Game situation

Emphasis: Offensive one-on-one behaviour with support of fellow players.

- **One-on-one with two passers at the penalty area line**

The two players stand opposite each other about 20-25 m from the penalty area. The attacker pushes through alone, or with the help of two passers who may only move on the boundary line of the 16-m-area. Shots at goal are executed both after individual actions and after co-operation with a neutral player.

Game situation

Emphasis: Pushing through alone in a one-on-one.

- **One-on-one alternating between two goals with two goalkeepers**

Two goals with two goalkeepers each are about 25-30 m apart. After the goalkick of a goalkeeper on one side the forward tries to push through against the defender in a one-on-one and to score a goal on the other side.

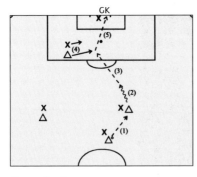

Game situation

Emphasis: One-on-one training after combination play.

- **One-on-one after a pass in the penalty area**

Outside the penalty area a free game three-on-three towards the goal takes place. From the combination game one of the three attackers tries to play to the forward in the penalty area. The latter must get away from the opponent with a brief acceleration, control the ball and take a shot at goal as quickly as possible.

2 Group Tactics

Group tactics covers all measures in which several players are involved. These include the defence, midfield and attack players. Tactical actions can occur both within and between these groups. The objective can be seen as getting tactical advantages from the particular situation in co-ordinated actions with fellow players.

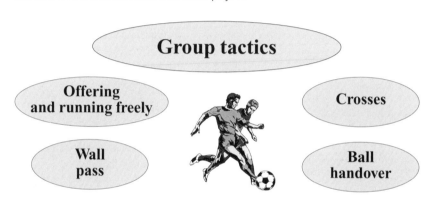

Group tactics

2.1 Offering and Running Freely

Offering and running freely

119

2.1.1 Tactical Conditions

Offering oneself and running freely are basic prerequisites for the success of combination play. Here the team-mate must get away from his opponent quickly in order to control the passed ball without disruption. Even without a pass, however, offering oneself and running freely is important from a group tactical point of view. By starting off in a certain direction one can "make room" for a team-mate for a successful action with the ball. In order to get tactical advantages from offering and running freely, the player must quickly assess a situation, react immediately and be capable of executing a highly intensive sprint.

(see following picture series)

Picture series offering and running freely

Group Tactics

2.1.2 Exercise and Game Forms

- Handball Game Five-on-five in a Marked-off Area
  By means of throwing, the ball should be kept in possession of one's own team for as long as possible.
  Special rules: A maximum of three steps may be run with the ball on the hand; no tipping the ball onto the ground; no body contact with the opponent. *Scoring:* Ten passes in a row to team-mates are rewarded with one point.

- Running into Space
  Two players pass the ball to each other at jogging speed at a distance of about 5 m.
  Variant A: The player in possession of the ball plays a through pass into the free area.
  Variant B: The player not in possession of the ball carries out a fast acceleration into the free area and in this way "demands" a through pass. In both situations the player getting away must control the ball as quickly as possible.

- Game 1 plus One-on-one
  A passer plays the ball to a fellow player who is closely marked by an opponent. He must get away from the opponent quickly, possibly after previous body feinting, and control the passed ball.

- Game One-on-one with Two Passers
  Starting situation as in the exercise above. Now, however, the free running player has the task of passing the controlled ball to a second passer after a one-on-one with the opponent. This procedure is repeated with a change of attack and defence player.

- Game 1 plus Four-on-four towards a Goal with Goalkeeper
  The player has the task of passing the ball from the back area to one of four attackers who are each covered closely by a defender. After previously getting away from the opponent, offering himself, running freely and a combination game amongst themselves the attackers try to score a goal. If the defenders get hold of the ball and, despite being harried, manage to get a pass through the attackers to a passer, this is evaluated as a point for the defence.

121

2.2 Wall Pass

Wall pass

2.2.1 Tactical Conditions

The wall pass is an appropriate tactical means of increasing the speed of one's own game and thus surprising the opponent. Use can be made of it in all parts of the team: playing out of one's own defence, bridging the midfield and carrying out an attack. The objective of the wall pass is always to reach the area behind the opposing defence players. This tactical variant occurs in a number of stages. Player A with the ball and his team-mate B ("wall player") are involved as follows:

- A recognises that in the current game situation the execution of a wall pass could be successful.
- A gets eye contact with wall player B who quickly gets away from his opponent and dashes towards the player with the ball.
- A passes the ball, after a short swinging back movement, with the inside or the outer instep, low, medium-hard and accurately to team-mate B.
- The ball bounces off the foot of player B "as from a wall" into the free area behind the opposing defence.
- After this surprise fast play-off, A sprints with explosive acceleration past his opponent and gets the low pass from the wall player under control.

The sequence of the wall pass can be seen in the photo series on page 123.

Picture series wall pass

In certain game situations *variants* of the wall pass are appropriate:

1. The opponent of the player with the ball recognises the intention of a wall pass and covers the area for the pass to the wall player.
   Variant: The player with the ball feigns a lay-off to the wall player past him on the other side.
2. The opponent of the wall player recognises the intention of a wall pass and covers the area for the pass back.
   Variant: The wall player feigns a "laying off" of the ball but instead controls it and dribbles it on the other side past the defender.
3. The wall player quickly gets away from his opponent after the pass back and dashes into the free space.
   Variant: A "double wall pass" is played by which the wall player directly gets the ball back from his team-mate after the pass back.

Soccer Tactics

2.2.2 Exercise and Game Forms

- **Pass to a Standing/Jogging Team-mate**
On a field about 20 m x 20 m eight players move with the ball. They dribble alternately towards one of four standing team-mates. From the dribbling comes a shot with the inside of the foot to a standing player who plays the pass back with the inside of his foot to where the original kicker runs with a brief acceleration after playing the ball. *Variations on the previous exercise:* Pass alternately with inside of the foot shots and/or outer instep shots with the right or left foot; the players previously standing now move at a slow running tempo.

- **Wall Pass with Two Wall Players**
An attacker dribbles towards a (active) defender. The person with the ball has the possibility of playing a wall pass with a wall player standing diagonally right or left of him and thus overcoming the defender.

- **Wall Pass or Dribbling with a Wall Player**
Variation on previous exercise: There is now only one wall player available. The attacker has the choice of outplaying the defender either with a wall pass or dribbling to the other side.

- **Wall Pass with Covered Wall Player**
An attacker again tries to outplay a defender with a wall pass. The wall player, however, is now covered by another defending player. A wall pass can now only succeed if the wall player can quickly get away from his opposing player in time, there is an accurate pass, the person who previously had the ball rapidly runs free and the pass back is precisely played to where he is running.

- **Situational Solution in a Game Two-on-two**
In order to overcome the defence the following tactical variants are possible: executed wall pass, dribbling instead of wall pass, feigned wall pass, double wall pass.

- **Game Three (4)-on-three (4) with Four Wall Players**
On a playing field about 15 m x 15 m with one wall player on each of four corners there are two teams of three/four. The person with the ball tries to carry out a wall pass with one of the four corner players in order to thus outplay his direct defender. After five successful wall passes the field and wall players change their positions. *Variations:* In

the three (4)-on-three (4) the persons involved can also play wall passes amongst themselves; each group of three/four may play wall passes either amongst themselves or with two particular diagonally opposite wall players.

- **Wall Pass in Attack and Counterattack**
  In free play four-on-four team A plays towards a normal goal with goalkeeper and team B when in ball possession towards two 5 m wide flag stick goals at the centre line. If a goal is scored after a previous wall pass this is counted double.

- **Wall Pass with Two Neutral Wall Players**
  Variation on previous exercise: On the right and left side lines are wall players who support the team in possession of the ball.

2.3 Ball Handover

Ball handover

2.3.1 Tactical Conditions

As with the wall pass, handing over the ball is a tactical means in order to irritate the opposite defence and gain advantages for structuring of the game. Such a ball handover to a team-mate can be useful in defence, midfield and also in attack. Player A with the ball and his team-mate B are involved in the sequence of this tactical variant in the following way:

- A recognises a favourable moment to execute a ball handover and gets eye contact with B.
- B then gets away from his opponent with a fast acceleration and dashes towards A.
- A shields the ball closely and lets his team-mate B take it over.

If the ball handover is to succeed, a number of things must be observed. The passing of the ball may only take place on the side where the ball is being moved: if A is moving the ball with his right foot, B must also take over the ball with his right foot and vice versa.

Furthermore the ball must be closely shielded with the body shortly before the handover and must under no circumstances be passed to the team-mate as otherwise safe moving of the ball would be disrupted. The sequence of the three different forms of ball handover can be seen in the photo series on page 127.

If player A with the ball and his partner B are running diagonally from different directions towards a defending player, the ball handover can be varied as follows:

1. B crosses the running path *in front of* A and in doing so takes over the ball *in front of* the body of his team-mate.

   (see photo series on page 127 (centre))

2. B crosses the running path *behind* A and in doing so takes over the ball *behind* the body of his team-mate.

   (see photo series on page 127 (below))

3. B crosses the running path *before* or *behind* A, only feigns a takeover, however, and A remains in possession of the ball.

Ball handover when running in opposite directions

*Ball handover when crossing **in front of** the team-mate*

*Ball handover when crossing **behind** the team-mate*

2.3 2 Exercise and Game Forms

- **Ball Handover when Running in Frontally Opposite Directions**
One player with and one without the ball run in a straight line towards each other and carry out a ball handover as they pass each other:
Variation: Move the ball alternately with the right and left foot.

- **Ball Handover in a Square**
One player with and five players without the ball move in a 10 m x 10 m square marked off with four flag sticks. After eye contact beforehand a ball handover is executed followed by dribbling around a flag stick.

- **Ball Handover when Running Diagonally in Opposite Directions**
One player with and one without the ball run diagonally towards each other and execute a ball handover at the point where their paths cross.
Variation: Ball handover in front of or behind the body of the team-mate.

- **Feigned Ball Handover**
Procedure as in the exercise above whereby the handover is only feigned and the person with the ball remains in possession.
Variation: Alternate between executed and feigned ball handover.

- **Ball Handover Followed by a Cross**
Two players on the wing run diagonally towards the goal to meet. First a ball handover is carried out, then, however, only feigned. After that the person with the ball crosses across the goal to the freely running team-mate who shoots or heads at goal.

- **Ball Handover Followed by an Attack**
Free play three (4)-on-three (4) in a 20 m x 20 m square at the centre line. After previous eye contact with the person currently in possession of the ball an additional player dashes from outside into the square and executes a ball handover and immediately follows the attack (four-on-three) towards the goal.

2.4 Crosses

Crosses

2.4.1 Tactical Conditions

If the attack game is to involve the wing positions, use is made of the cross. This procedure is recommended when attacks through the middle of the playing field are less successful and the opposing defence has weaknesses in defending high balls. One's own team must have good wingers who can cross as well as good headers among the forwards. Mastery of fast dribbles with many feints, secure inner instep shots as well as accurate headers or direct shots must be seen as technical prerequisites for this. The game via the wing is supported by including attacking full backs as flankers and midfield players moving up as additional attackers in front of the opponent's goal.

New goal opportunities should be constantly played out through crosses; this technical and tactical attack method should be varied in as diverse a way as possible:
1. By changing the trajectory of the ball through crossing the ball straight or with spin (away from the goal, towards the goal) and/or low, medium-high or high in front of the goal.
2. By changing proximity of the ball to the goal by crossing the ball either at the front or rear post, or close to or further away from the goal.

129

Photo series crosses

Group Tactics

2.4.2 Exercise and Game Forms

- **Crossing Changeover**
  Free play four-on-two on a field of about 15m x 15m. From the centre of play a long cross is made to an equally large field about 15-20m away. After previously offering himself, one of the four players there should receive the cross from the opposite zone. Those who cross are forced to kick accurately because another two defenders intervene.

- **Crossing and Running into Space**
  Free play four-on-two on a playing field between the side boundary of the penalty area and the sideline. About 20 m in front of the goal stands a forward. He then dashes in the direction of the goal when he recognises that one of the players can execute a cross. The forward receives the cross ball and executes a shot at goal .
  Variation: Two attackers dash into the penalty area and one defender tries to intercept the cross and stop a goal shot.

- **Cross in the Face of Opposition**
  Free play four-on-two on a playing field about 15 m x 15 m between the centre line and the sideline. If one of the players of the larger team dashes towards the goal via the wing, the defender currently standing closest to him follows him and tries to stop a cross into the penalty area. The other three members of the larger team run freely towards the goal where one of them receives the crossed ball in the face of opposition by the second defender and executes an attempt, shot or header, at goal.

- **Cross after Dribbling through a Stick Goal**
  Free play four-on-two from the centre line towards the goal. At the level of the penalty area boundary there is an approx. 5 m wide goal on both sides of the pitch. Only after first dribbling through one of these goals and a following cross from the right or left wing into the penalty area can one of the larger team players score a goal in the face of opposition.

- **Cross from a Side Zone**
  Free play four-on-two from the centre circle on a playing field from the extended side boundary of the penalty area to the centre. Outside this zone on the right and left wing there is one team-mate on each side. If he gets the ball from one of the four majority team players, he dribbles it to the level of the penalty area and executes an accurate cross to one of the attackers who has run with him. Again a goal is to be scored in the face of opposition by the two defenders after a long pass.

3 Team Tactics

Team tactics

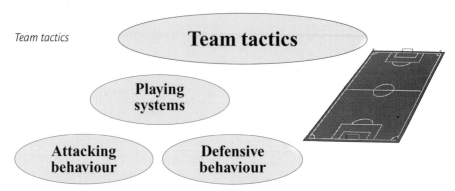

All individual and group tactical actions merge in the team together with game tactics, and combine in a game eleven-on-eleven. Thus the team tactics encompass all measures in defence and attack which are aimed at preventing or scoring goals. The game tactics chosen depend amongst other things on the following conditions: the current state of performance of one's own team, the current state of performance of the opponents, the place in the table, the kind of game (friendly, championship, cup), the location of the game (home, away), the current score, as well as the external conditions (size, type and state of pitch) including the weather (hot, cold, rain, wind). The basic components of team tactics are, however, the playing system, the attack and defence.

3.1 Playing Systems

The playing system serves to allocate each player in the team a certain position and task. This is not a matter of a rigid formation, however, as e.g. in volleyball. The positioning on the field taken up at the beginning of the game is later broken up as each player tries to fulfil the tasks which the system has given him. Not every playing system is equally suitable for every team. At the end of the day technical and tactical abilities of the players are the key for using a certain system. Since the beginnings of soccer over a century ago – also in relationship to the laws of the game – new playing systems have developed again and again. Today's way of playing is marked by the attempt to secure the area in front of the opponent's goal. If one's own team is in possession of the ball, the attackers are supported by the midfield players and also partly by the defenders moving up. From the diverse choice of current systems the 4:3:3 and the 3:5:2 systems will now be briefly discussed as an example.

The 4:3:3 system is often used in the youth and lower to mid amateur areas. It is characterised by a sweeper who forms the defence together with three backs. Three midfield players, distributed across the right, centre and left areas, are in the area between defence and attack. In attack there are three forwards. The filling of the right and left wing positions, as well as a centre forward, are characteristic of this system. In this way an offensive and also attractive way of playing is possible as the attacks not only take place through the centre but also increasingly via the wings.

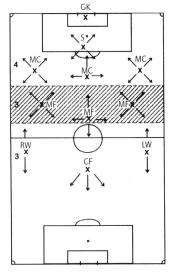

GK: Goalkeeper
S: Sweeper
MC: Man coverer
MF: Midfield player
RW: Right wing
LW: Left wing
CF: Centre forward

The 4:3:3 system

The 3:5:2 system is often used in the upper amateur and professional areas. It is characterised by the lack of a third attacker and the division of defence between a sweeper and two "man coverers". As a result the centre field is strongly occupied by five players to whom various and diverse tasks are allocated. Often the central position is occupied by a player whom the trainer allows freedom in the way he structures the game. Two mainly defensive, and two mainly offensive, players represent the link to the team's own defence and its own attack. Generally high demands are placed on the midfield players in this system in relationship to fitness and the variable technical and tactical tasks in attack and defence.

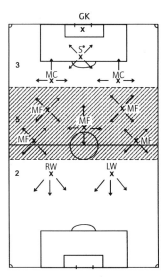

GK: Goalkeeper
S: Sweeper
MC: Man coverer
MF: Midfield player
RW: Right wing
LW: Left wing

The 3:5:2 system

3.2 Attack Behaviour

In the framework of team tactical attack behaviour the players must fulfil the following tasks in relationship to ball possession:

Ball possession:	Opponent's team	Own team
Attack behaviour:	Disruption of game build-up	Use of appropriate means of attack

If the opposing defence has intercepted an attack, the forwards must immediately take over defensive tasks. This includes running on in order to get back the lost ball. Furthermore the forwards try, together with the attacking midfield players, to restrict the opponent's room to build up a controlled attack. If one's own team has possession of the ball, the attacking players decide on the most promising means of attack. In doing so it is a good idea to include the midfield players in the attack in order to create superiority of numbers. In order to be able to play off one has to get away from the marking of the opponent. Getting away from the opponent by dashing into a free area is, however, not only important for one's own play-off. Also when you do not receive the ball you can create room to move for your team-mates through skillful free running. If you receive a pass you have to decide quickly whether it is better to carry out an individual action with the ball (dribbling, goal shot), a pass, cross or cooperative play (wall pass, ball handover). The final objective of team tactical attack behaviour remains the creation of goal opportunities for oneself or a team-mate.

3.3 Defence Behaviour

In the framework of team tactical defence behaviour the players must fulfil the following tasks in relationship to ball possession:

Ball possession:	Own team	Opponent's team
Defence behaviour:	Use of appropriate means of defence	Support of game build-up

If an opponent is in possession of the ball and starts an attack the defence must form quickly. This includes not allowing the attackers any superiority of numbers or space. The midfield players must strengthen the defence and "block" the areas in front of their own goal in order to prevent penetration by the opponent. Depending on the form of coverage, a particular opposing player is marked (man marking) or the forward who has penetrated a certain zone is attacked (area coverage).

The distance of the opponents from one's own goal decides whether distant or close coverage is to be carried out. Hereby the defence player must be conscious that a foul close to the goal could create advantages for the opponent through the possible awarding of a free kick or a penalty kick. From a tactical point of view the defence players must disturb the opposing forwards when they receive the ball, block their direct path to the goal and force them into an unfavourable position. Hindering goal success, and immediate gaining of the ball, are also the main tactical tasks of the defence which can occasionally be supported by setting up an off-side trap.

If the opponent's teamwork has been successfully disrupted and the defence is in possession of the ball, the build-up of an attack can be commenced. This in turn begins by the players offering themselves for the pass, for which purpose the defenders run freely in the corresponding areas. In this phase there is a switch from defence to attack which occurs quickly or with a delay, depending on tactical intentions. If your team is behind or plans a counterattack, the midfield must be quickly bridged with speedy dribbling, through passes or combination play with few ball contacts. If on the other hand the game is to be "drawn out", or the opponent is to be lured out of the mass of defence, the build-up of the game can be done slowly with dribblers holding onto the ball, diagonal and back passes. Technical ability and tactical discipline of the defence players are the prerequisites for putting such measures into effect.

III APPENDIX

1 External Factors Influencing Soccer Technique

How well a player masters the technique of his sport depends of course mainly on his own abilities. In addition, however, playing ability is also affected by a number of external factors. The following diagram shows the individual aspects.

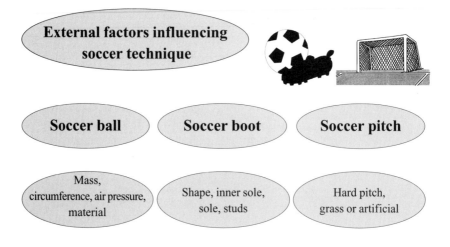

External factors influencing soccer technique

Here the first item to address is the soccer ball with its properties of mass, circumference, air pressure and material. But also the soccer boot and the soccer pitch with their peculiarities must be included in this subject area. Now the results of studies will be presented which will illustrate the close connection between the factors mentioned and soccer technique.

1.1 The Soccer Ball

Any experienced player can confirm that the peculiarities of the ball influence technique considerably. This applies especially to young people for whom enjoyment of the game and learning advances are very dependent on the quality of the ball material. The international soccer rules take this aspect into consideration, for the characteristics of the soccer ball are laid down within prescribed limits. Nevertheless, purely from feeling it is possible to state that even within the tolerance areas of the rules no one soccer ball is like another. There are results of an experimental study in the USA on this in which the characteristics of various soccer balls on impact at 68 km/h were analysed.

Influence of the Construction Type
Sealed balls had less mass, less maximum power and less impulses on impact than sewn balls. In addition their contact time and the time until reaching the highest power value were less. These differences can be attributed to the materials and the construction in each case.

Influence of Wetness
For balls of both types there were major increases in power and impulses in wetness, whereby those of the sewn balls were greater. Interestingly the time characteristics on impact were not changed by the influence of wetness.

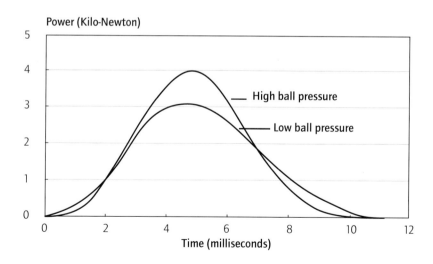

Power curves at impact of a ball with varying air pressure

Influence of Air Pressure

A variation of air pressure of balls within permitted limits changes their kicking characteristics quite considerably. The higher the air pressure, the greater are maximum power and impulse. At the same time, contact time and power increase time decrease. An example of this can be seen in the illustration on page 137.

In both curves shown on the graph the previously mentioned changes to kicking characteristics can be seen which arise purely from the variation of air pressure within the allowed limits. Such measurements are of great use. For one thing, they show through objective data how from time to time the characteristics of a soccer ball can be detected under certain conditions and thus influence technique. In addition such experiments, however, also pyrovide important information for the reduction of the risk of injury, e.g. in heading. For the protection of the health of a soccer player the selection of a ball must not take place purely under the aspect of playability, but must also include factors of the power-time characteristics on impact. In order to keep the danger of head injuries through the influence of the ball to a minimum, soccer clubs, the industry and research institutes must work together closely.

1.2 The Soccer Boot

The boot of a soccer player must meet a number of requirements: it must have an appropriate fitting form, allow playing the ball with feeling, and also be suited to running. The last named factor in particular is anything other than unimportant, for in a 90 minute game, a total of about 89 minutes is spent running and only one minute on actions with the ball! The importance of an individually fitting form of the soccer boot can be seen from the statistics according to which 70 per cent of the urban population has foot weaknesses. It is therefore not surprising that nearly all professional players require specially made soccer boots.

Often diverse experimental analyses are also carried out in connection with the design of a soccer boot. The following example places the emphasis on studies in five different areas:
- Measuring of the moving apparatus and the feet of soccer players
- Video analysis of the type and frequency of soccer-typical movements
- Kinematic analyses of movement processes in soccer
- Measurement of external forces between the ground and the boot
- Measurement of pressure distribution in the boot on selected areas of the foot sole.

According to these extensive studies a soccer boot should have the following characteristics:

➤ When selecting a soccer boot not only the length (size) but also various foot diameters and instep heights should be considered.
➤ Through the fitting form a functional unity of foot and boot must be ensured.
➤ When designing the boot, the soccer-typical major load on the toes must be taken into consideration.
➤ The central area of the foot must have a high degree of flexibility.
➤ The heel must be made in such a way that there is no rubbing of the Achilles' tendon and the ankles.
➤ The tongue must have both stiffness (for the shot) and flexibility to distribute forces working on the foot.
➤ The sole must resist extreme torsion, maintain stability and functionally work together with the studs.

➤ The distribution of screw-on studs varies, usually four or five are placed at the front (sometimes with differing lengths and angles) and two in the rear.
➤ The inner sole must have both a shock absorbing effect as well as being elastic, it therefore usually consists of two different materials.

1.3 The Soccer Pitch

The last factor to be considered is the soccer pitch with its varying surfaces. The characteristics of a cinder pitch, natural or artificial grass, have an undisputed influence on technique. The player must adjust his movements to the particular surface. The bouncing behaviour of the ball is also different on the sport surfaces mentioned. The current situation of the pitch, whether well-prepared or much played on, dry or wet, places additional demands on the player's technique. Comprehensive experimental studies on the characteristics of cinder, natural and artificial pitches were carried out by the Institute for Biomechanics of the German Sport University in Cologne. To observe the characteristics of the ground properties, football-typical starting, stopping and turning movements were carried out with the same boots. The following results, among others, were achieved:

➤ The static friction coefficient proved to be a fitting characteristic for the description of the peculiarities of a particular ground.
➤ The static friction characteristics of the ground considerably influence the execution of movements.
➤ A high level of friction allows good starting and stopping, but strains the moving apparatus more.
➤ It is not possible to allocate a constant friction coefficient to a particular ground for this is dependent on the type of movement. Thus for one player the cinder ground was more dull than the artificial ground when stopping; when starting, however, it was the other way round.
➤ On the cinder ground a sudden braking is possible with one step because of the long sliding distance. On the artificial ground, however, either a major bending at the knees or a stuttering stop with several steps is necessary.
➤ Turning movements on dull ground require greater unloading for which the body must be raised higher with the use of more energy.
➤ The heavier a player is, the higher his friction coefficient is on all grounds studied. Qualitatively this results in a different load form than for a lighter player.
➤ In tests to reach a greatest possible jumping height it turned out that these are much better on artificial grounds than on cinder grounds.

In conclusion it can be seen here that on differing ground in each case individual adaptation is necessary. An improvement or deterioration of friction can be achieved both through the choice of appropriate footwear (studs) and through adjusting movement (technique).

2 Application Areas for Experimental Analyses

Finally we will show here which research techniques and methods can be used in various areas of sport soccer to attain further findings. In the form of a brief overview the following illustration lists the four areas discussed.

Application areas for experimental analyses in soccer

Technique	Fitness	Load	Physique
– Movements without the ball	– Strength	– External forces	– Proportions
– Movements towards the ball	– Speed	– Internal forces	– Height
– Movements with the ball	– Endurance	– Injuries	– Mass

Application areas for experimental analyses

2.1 Technique

Here only short additions are required as this book has already mentioned a number of analyses. Use of video devices should be emphasised again, which are useful in many ways: whether for determining tactical aspects, in match analyses with details of

Devices for video digitalisation

141

frequency and effectiveness of certain actions or in the framework of movement analyses. In comparison to other games there are obviously deficits in this connection in soccer.

2.2 Fitness

The important biomotor abilities of an athlete include the factors strength, speed and endurance. There are numerous possibilities for exactly ascertaining the state of performance of a soccer player in this connection. Here one relies less on one's own personal feeling and trusts more in the objective informational ability of certain devices. This procedure can require effort, but it provides the coach with reliable information on the current performance capacity of his players.

2.2 .1 Strength

In one-on-ones in particular, but also in jumps, fast accelerations and movements with the ball, the soccer player needs well-developed strength abilities. In training, these performance components can be improved through gymnastics, exercises with small equipment or on special strength training machines. A rough checking of the current state of strength can be carried out e.g. by determining the height reached in vertical jumps, the height of hurdles jumped over, or the distance of horizontal jumps. If the player carries out running or jumping movements on a power measuring platform, findings can be gathered from the signal received both on the forces in various directions and also on velocity and the path of the body's centre of gravity.

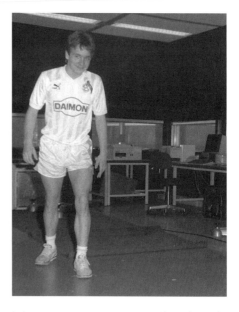

Laboratory measurement to determine the dynamics of a fast acceleration

The effectiveness of various training forms or gymnastic exercises can be checked with the aid of electromyography. Here conclusions are drawn from the action potentials of the working muscles about the training stimuli connected with them. In this way help can be given in choosing player-specific exercise forms. Thus it was found that amongst several players certain exercises in no way created the same, but rather varying degrees of activity of the muscles. Furthermore minor changes to the body position in exercise repeats led to muscular stimuli which varied greatly from each other. Such measurements are used both in regular competitive training and also in build-up training after injuries.

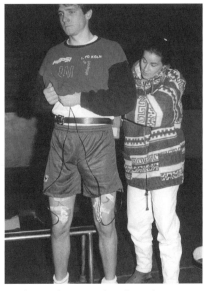

Putting on the measuring electrodes

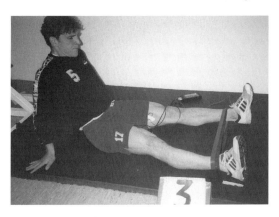

EMG measurement in a strengthening exercise

2.2.2 Speed

Recently speed has developed as a biomotor performance factor of high significance. Therefore exercise and game forms for improving, and tests for checking speed, should be part of every long-term training programme. Determining running time with a mechanical stopwatch can, however, only be reliable over longer running distances of more than 50 m. To measure soccer-typical speed over distances of 5 m, 10 m, 20 m or 30 m on the other hand, electronic light barriers or ultra sound velocity measurement should be used.

2.2.3 Endurance

The high running demands linked with one-on-ones and actions with the ball require good endurance performance capacity of the soccer player. For this purpose the ability to quickly overcome fatigue after highly intensive movements must be acquired in training. Videographic running distance analyses give the coach information on running distances covered. Reliable conclusions about the current state of performance of a player, as well as the effect of certain training measures in relation to endurance, can also be made from lactate measurements. Such examinations are routinely carried out in the area of professional soccer. The less complicated determining of heart rate on the other hand is not considered a reliable criterion for determining endurance performance capacity.

2.3 Load

In almost all soccer movements, external forces affect the player. They are transmitted to the inside of the body in bones, muscles, tendons and ligaments, and can have a positive or negative effect. The following graph gives an insight into the significance of maximum forces in a number of soccer-typical movements.

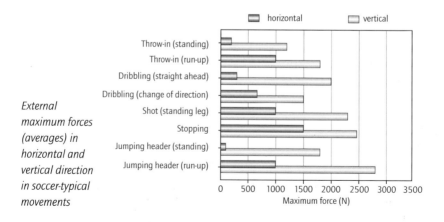

External maximum forces (averages) in horizontal and vertical direction in soccer-typical movements

Highest values in the horizontal running direction result from sudden stopping when running. In the vertical direction, ground reaction forces of an average 2800 N (about 280 Kilopond) occur in a two-legged jump-off or a jumping header. In biomechanical analyses the effect of such forces on the moving apparatus are examined. From this recommendations for practical situations can be deduced.

In training the human body adapts to mechanical stimulus. It reacts to doses which are too high with a reduction of tissue which in the long-term is expressed in damage through wear and tear e.g. reduction of the joint cartilage. Thus a training structure which is matched to the biological prerequisites of the player is extremely important. To avoid injuries the following recommendations can be given: reduce training intensity if pains occur, reduce bending and turning loads, take previous injuries into consideration and avoid hard kicks. Early development of sport-specific techniques, a good training state, sufficient warming-up, suitable equipment and matching of training demands to the current performance state of the player also have a preventive effect.

2.4 Physique

An analysis of the player's physique is useful in many respects for the proportions of the body are major influencing factors with regard to technique, fitness and also load. For this, measurements are necessary which determine the height, proportions and weight. These data describe the type of physique and serve as a basis for calculating model factors such as component masses and moments of inertia. Compared with participants in other sports, the physique of soccer players cannot be considered homogeneous. Rather it involves a medium, normally athletically developed type in which the relevant movement characteristics endurance, speed, strength (power) and dexterity can be optimally combined.

Legende

Defence player	X
Attack player	△
Goalkeeper	X △ GK GK
Passer	⊗
Player in possession of the ball	₀X
Player in straddle situation	Λ
Running path **Sequence of running path**	⟶ 1 (2, 3)
Pass, cross, shot at goal **Sequence of pass, cross, shot at goal**	– – – – – – → 1 (2, 3)
Dribbling	∿∿∿→
Small goal made of flag sticks	⚑ ⚑

Bibliography

ASAMI, T. et al: Analysis of Movement Patterns of Referees during Soccer Matches. In: Science and Football, London 1988, 341-345.

BAUER, G.: Richtig Fußballspielen. München 1996.

BAUMANN, W.: Belastungen des Bewegungsapparates bei sportlichen Bewegungen. In: Leistungssport 19 (1989) 3, 2.

BISANZ, G./VIETH, N. (Hrsg.): Fußball von morgen, Grundlagen- und Aufbautraining. Münster 1995.

GROSSER, M./NEUMAIER, A.: Techniktraining, Theorie und Praxis aller Sportarten. München 1982.

INSTITUT FÜR BIOMECHANIK: Biomechanische Untersuchung an Kunststoffrasenflächen und Sportschulen für Fußball und Hockey. Forschungsbericht Köln 1986.

KOLLATH, E.. Bewegungsanalyse in den Sportspielen. Köln 1996.

LEVENDUSKY, T.A.: Impact Characteristics of Two Types of Soccer Ball under a Variety of Conditions. Southern Methodist University, Dallas (USA) 1987.

RODANO, R./COVA, P./VIGANO, R.: Designing a Football Boot: a Theoretical and Experimental Approach. In: Science and Football. London 1988, 416-428.

SUZUKI, S. et al: Analysis of the Goalkeeper's Diving Motion. In: Science and Football. London 1988, 468-475.

YAMANAKA, K. et al: Time and Motion Analysis in Top Class Soccer Games. In: Science and Football. London 1988, 334-340.

More Soccer!

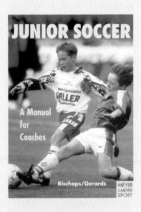

Klaus Bischops/
Heinz-Willi Gerards
**Coaching Tips
for Children's Soccer**

Coaching Tips for Children's Soccer is a complete guide for ensuring that young players get the most out of the game – psychologically, socially and physically. Starting with the belief that fun and self discovery are the most important aspects of any sporting activity for children up to the age of 10, **Coaching Tips for Children's Soccer** covers the basic principles of child development and details 60 play-oriented training units which can be utilised by teachers, parents and others working with this age group.

128 pages, 10 photos, 3 figures
paperback, 11.5 x 18 cm
ISBN 3-89124-529-7
£ 5.95 UK/$ 8.95 US/$ 12.95 Cdn

Klaus Bischops/
Heinz-Willi Gerards
Junior Soccer
A Manual for Coaches

In this book soccer coaches and teachers will find around 100 complete training units for youth-work in clubs. Each unit contains a warm-up section, a section on the main emphasis in the training unit and a specific "winding-down" section with a game. The book begins with the training units for 5-10 year-old children and ends with suggestions for the teenagers (age 16-18). An appendix gives useful hints on questions of organisation, team spirit and social events.

168 pages, 29 photos, 70 figures
paperback, 14.8 x 21 cm
ISBN 1-84126-000-2
£ 12.95 UK/$ 17.95 US/$ 25.95 Cdn

MEYER & MEYER Verlag | Von-Coels-Straße 390 | D-52080 Aachen | Fax ++49 (0)2 41/9 58 10-10

More Soccer!

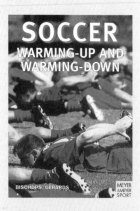

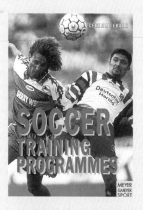

Gerhard Frank
**Soccer
Training Programmes**

Klaus Bischops/
Heinz-Willi Gerards
**Soccer – Warming-up
and Warming-down**

In this book the authors provide some 35 programmes for proper warming-up and warming-down for soccer. The programmes are full of variety to avoid monotony and are based around the game of soccer itself, within a team situation. The book is ideal for coaches and trainers involved in the wellbeing of a soccer team, from youngsters to veterans. The authors present their ideas in a manner that can be easily grasped and understood by everyone involved in the game.

136 pages, 22 photos, 172 figures
paperback, 14.8 x 21 cm
ISBN 1-84126-014-2
£ 8.95 UK/$ 14.95 US/$ 20.95 Cdn

Soccer Training Programmes contains a collection of 96 detailed plans designed to be used by amateur coaches. In clear and concise chapters **Soccer Training Programmes** also provides an overview of the key aspects of a coach's work, including physical training, skill development, tactics and psychological preparation. Other features of the book include a valuable discussion of periodisation for soccer, a special section on supplementary indoor training activities and an appendix of stretching exercises.

216 pages
numerous photos and figures
paperback, 14.8 x 21 cm
ISBN 3-89124-556-4
£ 12.95 UK/$ 17.95 US/$ 25.95 Cdn

08/00

MEYER & MEYER Verlag | Von-Coels-Straße 390 | D-52080 Aachen | Fax ++49 (0)2 41/9 58 10-10